Wall Street's
JUST
NOT
THAT INTO
YOU

Wall Street's
JUST
NOT
THAT INTO
YOU

An Insider's Guide to
Protecting and Growing Wealth

ROGER C. DAVIS

bibliomotion
inc.

First published by Bibliomotion, Inc.
39 Harvard Street
Brookline, MA 02445
Tel: 617-934-2427
www.bibliomotion.com

ISBN: 978-1-62956-117-2, print
ISBN: 978-1-62956-118-9, ebook
ISBN: 978-1-62956-119-6, enhanced ebook

(CIP data applied for)

Dedicated to
my wife, Joy,
and our children,
Grace and Clayton

CONTENTS

Contents

CHAPTER ONE

A Confidence Crisis

"It's all a crapshoot."
—Fred Craig—

ON SEPTEMBER 7, 2001, an important client called my office and instructed me to liquidate his account. He didn't have a particular reason for doing so; he just felt unsettled. Having been trained in the Wall Street way, I encouraged him not to sell any of the quality investments in his account and rehashed all the reasons I'd been taught to never sell equity investments.

Despite my best efforts to dissuade this client from making a rash move prompted by little more than an uneasy feeling, he was resolute. I followed his instructions.

I'd gone to work as a stockbroker for Dean Witter in 1992. When I came back from training at the company headquarters in the World Trade Center in New York, I was armed and dangerous. This client was a contractor, and one of the most highly regarded custom homebuilders in Mississippi. He was also my stepfather and a man I admired greatly. We had a great relationship, and he had a sharp wit. The first thing my stepfather, Fred, said to me upon my arrival in Mississippi was, "It's all a crapshoot." He said that to me over and over again, and I hated it.

Investing in the market was a crapshoot as far as Fred was concerned. He viewed Wall Street as the house and the public as the players. I couldn't stand it, but that didn't stop him from saying it. "It's just a crapshoot," he would say, whether we were making money or losing money—it didn't matter which.

The reason I hated hearing it was that deep down I feared he was right. The way I'd been trained to buy and hold investments for clients with little regard for what was going on in the market had never sat well with me, but I didn't know any other way to do it. My entire career up to that point had been in a bull market, so when they said "buy the dips," it had always worked.

Well, it worked until it stopped working. The long-term bull market that had been in place since 1982 ended in mid-2000, but even in the wake of the 9/11 attacks, Wall Street's advice was to "stay the course." As the market continued to decline, I became increasingly uncomfortable acting as little more than a cheerleader for my clients and the market. If the market was really just a crapshoot, we were on one heck of a bad run, and I wanted to change tables.

Even if Fred couldn't put his finger on why he felt the way he did, one thing was for sure: he was out of the market two trading days before 9/11.

So I began my *real* education about markets, risk, and opportunity. If the market was a crapshoot, then I wanted to improve my odds. If there were people who knew a better way of doing things than Wall Street's "Buy, Hold, and Hope" method, I was sure going to find them.

The investment community seems to be split into two distinct groups.

The Buy-and-Hold Investors

The largest group is the one that believes successful investing is predicated on investing in a diverse set of investments and holding them for a very long time. This group emphasizes financial planning, asset allocation, and diversification.

Given sufficient time, the stock market has always gone to new highs, and therefore owning the market long-term is the best course of action—at least according to this first group. Rather than focus on which investments to make and how best to time those investments, they focus on establishing an asset allocation based on the investor's age, time frame, and tolerance for risk. There is an emphasis on client goals and a reliance on the markets (the investment allocation) to achieve those goals over the long term.

The Tactical Investors

The second and much smaller group tends to focus on making tactical investments given current market conditions, the availability of favorable investment opportunities, and risk management. Tactical investors generally aren't content with just taking whatever return the market provides. They favor investment systems—trend-following systems and counter-trend systems, to name just two.

While the market has always ultimately made higher highs, this group would point out that there have been long periods during which the market has produced little or even negative returns. Tactical investors are interested in generating positive returns even when the markets are in decline.

These Two Groups Have Been Largely Incompatible

Buy-and-hold investors simply don't believe that performance can be improved by security selection or trend analysis. Planning and long-term investing is the key to success, they would say.

Tactical investors can't imagine why buy-and-hold investors would continue to own investments that decline 50 percent and more. They believe there is no riskier proposition than investing in the market as a buy-and-hold investor with little or no sell discipline.

What Am I?

In the early part of my twenty-plus-year investment career, having been trained by Wall Street firms, I found myself in the buy-and-hold camp. But as the markets began to unravel in the early 2000s, I became increasingly uncomfortable with the methods I'd been taught and had advocated. I had a confidence crisis.

The eighteen months from March 7, 2000, through September 11, 2001, were a period of great learning for me. As the S&P 500 was peaking in the first few weeks of March 2000, I was focused on the birth of my first child and was paying little attention to the market or my personal investments. By the time I re-engaged, my investment account was down several hundred thousand dollars.

Because I had been weaned on the "buy-and-hold" mentality, I stayed the course. Conventional wisdom told me to hold on, so that's exactly what I did.

Then something extraordinary happened. Within a matter of months, the company I worked for got bought out. As a result of the buyout, I had more than $1 million. Keep in mind that this was a time when it was difficult to make and protect money in the market, and there I was, thirty years old and sitting on a small fortune. I had lost even more money in my investment account, but within months I'd made it all back—because I was in the right place at the right time. But the sudden windfall had nothing to do with making quality investment decisions or the buy-and-hold motto. If anything, adhering so religiously to this philosophy kicked me when I was already down.

Then, the very next year, the World Trade Center's twin towers fell. In the immediate aftermath of the 9/11 attacks on our country, the stock market closed for four days, reopening on September 17th. Those days were long ones for every American as we contemplated the tragic loss of life, wondering if anything would ever be the same again.

One of the things I remember about that time was the investment advice coming from Wall Street. It was the same old song—"Buy, Hold, and Hope"—and the lyrics hadn't changed. Wall Street was telling people exactly what they had told me: "Sit tight and don't worry. Things will work out okay in the end." There was even the strong implication that to reduce exposure to stocks was somehow unpatriotic.

In 2006, I left a big Wall Street firm and started a Registered Investment Advisory company with three partners. We started the company with the idea that not losing money in bear markets made it a lot easier to make money in bull markets. Since starting the company, we've seen another huge cyclical bear market that hurt buy-and-hold investors even worse than the dot-com crash. Our systems protected our clients from much of the pain in 2008–2009. Today, markets are at record levels again. Despite the hard lessons the market has taught investors in recent years, many have the same unprotected exposure to the market that they had in 2000 and in 2007. A major difference in the situation investors find themselves in today is that, unlike in the previous two declines, a bubble now exists in bonds. The government has already done just about all it can do to prop up the economy and the markets.

While our focus has been on the investment management part of the business (which I consider to be the most important), in the last several years I've begun to appreciate that financial planning is valuable to wealthy families. I've come to believe that, rather than being mutually exclusive, these two philosophies are quite complementary.

This book illuminates my efforts to combine the best elements of both of these philosophies: Tactical portfolio management

I've come to believe that, rather than being mutually exclusive, these two philosophies are quite complementary.

in conjunction with robust goal setting and planning truly is a rational approach to charting your financial future.

There is no absolute right and absolute wrong in investing, but there is wisdom in assessing current market conditions and prevailing trends within the context of an investor's long-term goals.

In this book, I'll map out that wisdom, guiding you toward the investment choices that are right for you.

CHAPTER TWO

Aren't You Done with the Roller Coaster?

"If the shoeshine guy is giving stock tips,
the market is overvalued."
—Joe Kennedy, summer 1929—

ACCORDING TO YOUR average Wall Street firm, investing is, if not exactly easy, then at least simple. It all comes down to a relatively basic series of steps:

1. Develop a financial goal.
2. Assess the tolerance for risk (that is, determine the acceptable level of volatility).
3. Evaluate the client's time frame.
4. Consider the historical return and correlation ratios of various asset classes and invest in

> **The only thing about the future that we can predict with any degree of certainty is the fact that it will be different from the past. You might say that the future and the past are like cousins—there's a resemblance.**

a portfolio of funds that, in hindsight, *would* have accomplished the financial goal articulated in Step 1.

5. Hold on tight to these investments *for the long term* on the strength of their historical performance. Do this no matter what happens.

This strategy is not terrible, and it has some solid attributes, but there are significant problems with it as well. First, the future will be different from the past. While the future will have things in common with the past, it will unfold in ways that are impossible to predict. The only thing about the future that we can predict with any degree of certainty is the fact that it will be different from the past. You might say that the future and the past are like cousins—there's a resemblance.

Second, this approach overemphasizes those issues unique to the investor. Considerable weight should be given to the investor's timeline, needs, and limitations when developing an investment strategy. It is certainly important to know these things, but they are only part of the puzzle.

The condition and direction of the current market must influence the tactical investment decisions. An advisor must have a finger on the pulse of the market and have an up-to-date understanding of the current economic climate—things that exist independent of the client and his or her financial goals. **The stock and bond markets do not exist to provide for an individual's retirement. The market is utterly indifferent to the individuals who participate in it.**

Like a recipe, the ingredients of a well-positioned portfolio (goals, risk tolerance, and timeline, as well as market conditions and asset characteristics) have to be portioned correctly. A teaspoon of sugar is delicious; a cupfull is disgusting. There is a "sweet spot," if you will, where all of those factors are considered and we can make credible decisions based on the current reality rather than memories of the past, imaginings of the future, or simply blind hope.

> **Like a recipe, the ingredients of a well-positioned portfolio (goals, risk tolerance, and time-line, as well as market conditions and asset characteristics) have to be portioned correctly. A teaspoon of sugar is delicious; a cupfull is disgusting.**

The third major problem with Wall Street's approach is the "buy-and-hold" mantra that we hear so often. Traditional advisors would have investors accept any level of fluctuation in the value of their investments for the promise that it might all pay off in the end. I like to call this "the roller coaster ride of a lifetime."

Parts of a roller coaster ride are fun and exciting; there are (quite literally) great highs. But roller coasters aren't nearly as much fun as they're supposed to be. They actually hurt; they jerk you around, banging you into hard metal on one side and a stranger on the other. There are thrilling moments, but for the most part all they really offer is good old-fashioned nausea. Then, there are terrible periods when you are tossed around helplessly, feeling that sickening dread in the pit of your stomach. The thing about roller coasters, however, is that no matter how many hills and valleys there are, you always wind up back where you started. That's what a buy-and-hold investment strategy feels like in a long-term bear market.

What if you could smooth out the nerve-wracking periods without reducing the upside potential? What if you could end the ride in a better position than where you started?

The guiding principle of our investment philosophy is a close, dispassionate observation of the market. Markets trend. Individual stocks trend; sectors of the market and global markets trend much of the time. These trends can be observed and recorded, and we can glean critical information from them. **Investing alongside those trends and not against them is an essential part of our investment process.**

Look at the price charts for these markets:

DOW JONES 1921-1929

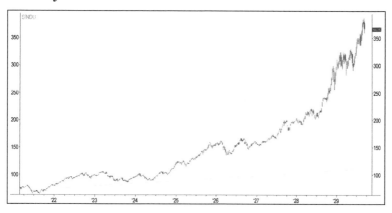

DOW JONES 1929-1932

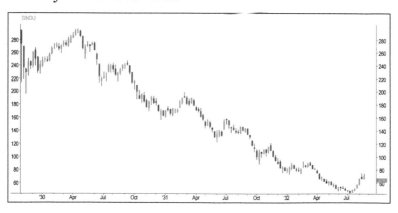

Source: TradeStation

NASDAQ 1985-2014

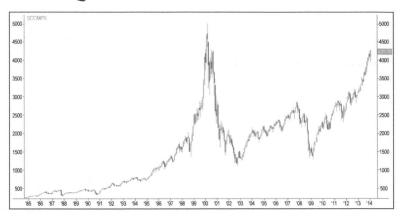

LATIN AMERICA 2004-late 2007

Source: TradeStation

Whatever you choose, you will see clear price trends. Those prices are not just bouncing around randomly; they behave in a predictable fashion, and if you know what to look for, you can profit from the uptrends and avoid the downtrends. This is why I think the most important question investors or advisors should be asking is, *What is the market doing right now and how does that relate to the recent past?*

An investor can save a great deal of money and heartache if he understands how the market is trending. Trends are identifiable and quantifiable, and they last long enough that if you invest alongside them you can achieve far greater investment success. And by heeding evidence of a changing trend, you can preserve your capital and not get caught flatfooted by a market downturn.

In general, the buy-and-hold community is not in favor of this type of informed flexibility. Instead, Wall Street has what could be called a "permanent bull market bias." They essentially operate as though markets were perpetually in the midst of a bull market. You'll notice that few investment firms ever really describe the market as risky, except in the fine print of their sales literature. When have you ever heard a Wall Street analyst say, "We see the market 25 percent lower a year from now?" Rarely do their investment opinions account for the potential downturn.

Experience, however, tells us that there are periods of time—sometimes quite lengthy periods of time—when stocks go down. In just the past thirteen years, we've had two stock market declines of about 50 percent! Most people have a general sense of the difference between a bull and bear market, but there are a number of misconceptions about how these markets function and how long they last—and some on Wall Street nurture these misunderstandings because it suits their business model.

The fact is that the market goes through very long-term (some might say "secular") bull and bear markets. These *can* last twenty years or more. If you look at a market in a historical context, you can clearly see that certain market conditions are frequently maintained for years on end.

We are currently in a long-term bear market, and have been since 2000. The previous secular bull market began in 1982 and ended in 2000. A price chart from 1982–2000 demonstrates that although the market did suffer setbacks, it generally supported higher prices. The DOW Jones (see below), for example, went from approximately 1,000 in 1982 to 11,000 in 2000.

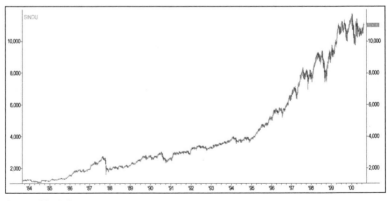

Source: TradeStation

In this sort of atmosphere—a long-term bull market— a buy-and-hold strategy makes sense. You maintain your investments through small downturns with an expectation of higher returns in the future. It is perhaps not ideal, but buying a diverse set of investments and hanging on to them works reasonably well in that sort of market.

If you look further back, however, at the period from 1966 to 1982, the DOW Jones went from 1,000 to 1,000.

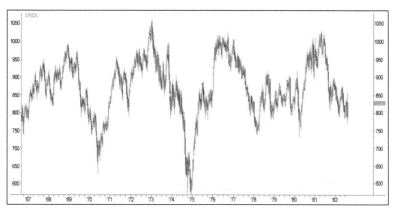

Source: TradeStation

That's sixteen years during which buy-and-hold investors made little or no money. That's not to say that there was no opportunity to profit during those sixteen years—far from it. Nor does it imply that Dow 1,000 in 1966 to Dow 1,000 in 1982 was simply flat. In fact the returns were:

1. -25%   4. +66%   7. -27%

2. +32%   5. -45%   8. +40%

3. -36%   6. +75%   9. -24%

In that sort of market climate, the buy-and-hold philosophy doesn't make any sense and can leave you frustrated or broke.

A bull market is characterized by rising asset prices. Now, in a bull market there will likely be setbacks—such as the 1987 crash, or the 1998 "Asian contagion," when the US markets were hit with fallout from the East Asian economic crisis. The stock market will occasionally take a beating, even in a bull market. What makes it a bull market, however, is the fact that, overall, the market trends upward.

But the long-term bear market is not the simple inverse of the bull market. If you were to draw a graph of a bull market, you would wind up with a solidly up-sloping line, but if you were to draw a graph of a bear market, it would look more like a series of huge peaks and deep valleys. A bear market is not a straightforward descent, but rather a period of dramatic moves, both up and down, that leave you right back where you started—just like the roller coaster. A long-term bear market is characterized by sharp declines followed by several years of nice gains, followed in turn by another sharp decline. This cycle can repeat itself over and over until the long-term bear market concludes.

Imagine it's the year 2000. You've just inherited $2 million of General Electric. Your grandfather bought it many years before and never sold a share. The stock is trading at $50 when the estate settles in March of 2000, and you receive 40,000 shares into your account. The stock trades up to $60 by September of 2000, tacking on another $400,000 to the value of your investment account. In March of 2001, the stock trades as low as $36 a share; you are uncomfortable, but remember that, like your grandfather, you are a long-term investor. A few months later, GE trades back into the low $50s and you secretly consider selling it when it gets back to $60, where it had been nine months before.

Now, with the benefit of hindsight, we know that the stock hasn't traded higher than the low $40s since 2001, and it traded as low as $5.73 a share in March of 2009. At its lowest price, what had been $2.4 million in GE stock was worth $229,000. Ouch! Of course the stock is at $27 today, up more than 370 percent from the bottom; but that makes your 40,000 shares worth $1,080,000, or 55 percent less than the peak value.

Would it have been helpful to know that the long-term market structure would change from bull to bear in late 2000/early 2001? If you had known that long-term bull and bear markets often last ten to twenty years, would your decision-making process have been affected? I hope so. Founded by Thomas Edison, General Electric is one of the most successful and widely recognized companies in American business history. Every house in the country has products made by General Electric, and old dividend-paying stocks are supposed to be safe, right? And yet stockholders who bought in

2000 are still down 55 percent in 2014. In my opinion, you would have to be in a coma to accept that level of volatility without some pretty potent sedatives.

The S&P 500 went up almost 100 percent from 2003—when the market bottomed after the dot-com bubble—through 2007 (see below), when it briefly reclaimed the highs of 2000. There was a lot of money to be made by owning stocks then, and many investors did very well.

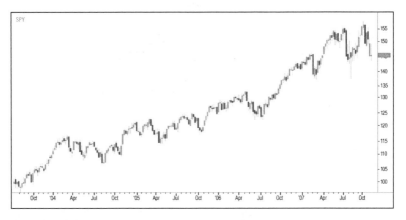

Source: TradeStation

Then, from October 2007 to March of 2009, the S&P 500 plummeted 56 percent (see following page).

That wiped out all the gains of the previous few years and then some. You can chart this sort of thing in any bear market: a big sell-off followed by very nice gains, repeated until the larger secular cycle turns over. For this reason, we say that every secular market also contains a number of smaller

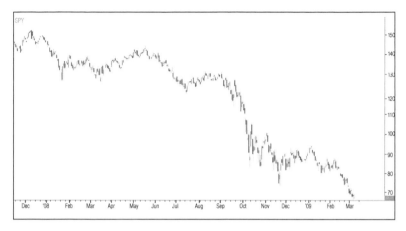

Source: TradeStation

cyclical bull and bear markets. Though we have been in a bear market for the past fourteen years, there was a big cyclical bull market from 2003 to 2007 and another from March 2009 until today.

Understanding what sort of long-term market we are in—and what sort of smaller cycle is going on inside it—can make the difference between successfully investing in a down market and losing half your wealth by "holding for the long term." Just because you are ready to retire, just because you've done everything that Wall Street told you to do, just because you have diversified your portfolio and allocated your funds according to their principles, doesn't mean that the market will reward you. A serious decline in the market will wreck even the best-laid plans if you're not ready for it. Remember, the market is indifferent to your financial goals.

Remember, the market is indifferent to your financial goals.

All of this goes to show that an approach founded on a bull-market bias is seriously flawed. Essentially, it amounts to a denial of reality. A typical Wall Street strategy would have you ignore these very real downturns and invest the very same way in November of 2007 as you should in April 2009.

It's a continuing puzzle to me just how static the approach to investing can be, especially when it comes to investors with serious wealth. All too often I've seen families with $100,000,000 and families with $250,000 being offered virtually the same investment program. The philosophy and approach doesn't appear to change, even for the investor who has four, five, or twenty-five times as much as the typical investor. Of course, they're not completely identical. A program designed for a wealthier investor may be dressed up, priced differently, or given a few more bells and whistles, but when you get right down to the basic functioning of the investments, the diversification of assets, it's all pretty much the same.

Most investment firms have a limited set of "tools" in their arsenal. Asset allocation and diversification, for example, are the go-to methods for managing risk, no matter who the client is and what the current environment requires. I believe a more dynamic, sophisticated investment philosophy, one that isn't wholly dependent on rising stock and bond prices to be successful, is more appropriate for today's investors.

This is not to say that a tactical investment firm that follows trends (like ours) will get in at the bottom and out at the top. Trend followers are not trendsetters, after all; we need to have a few early adopters to follow. Nor does it suggest that our clients won't experience drawdowns (a decline in the value of their account), because they do. The advisor's job is to minimize the impact of drawdowns by recognizing patterns of market behavior and investing accordingly. And if you get the predominant trend of the market right—even just mostly right—it solves a lot of the major problems with investing.

Let us return, then, to that fictional roller coaster. A roller coaster can be a fun novelty, but it's no way to really get anywhere. And though it may be thrilling for five minutes, you probably don't want to spend five hours riding the dips and curves. My goal is to give you the tools to get you off that roller coaster and back on solid ground, in an environment where *you* control how fast you go and how much risk you're comfortable taking.

Investing is always a roller coaster to some degree. You can't control the markets—no one can. But you *can* decide when and where to get off the ride. The key is to make the right investments using the right information. In other words, although you're not the one operating the roller coaster, you still have control over how you ride.

CHAPTER THREE

Wall Street's One-Size-Fits-All Approach

"Often wrong but never in doubt."

—Ivy Baker Priest—

OVER THE YEARS, Wall Street has become adept at selling its approach—it has to be, because the virtues of the buy-and-hold roller coaster are far from self-evident. With the vast majority of advisors using this model, it's not surprising that so many otherwise astute people stick with an investment philosophy that doesn't help them. They simply don't know how to do it differently.

The financial media is not in the business of making you wealthy or helping you secure the wealth you already have. The financial media is just that: media. The primary objective for any media outlet is the sale of ad space, and the content of everything from *Squawk Box* to *Seinfeld* is geared toward getting as many eyes as possible on that ad space. A TV show may be artistically significant, but in a very real way its primary goal is simply to be attractive. It exists to draw in the largest possible percentage of the target market. The same goes for financial magazines. If the choice is between helpful and exciting, the media will choose exciting every time.

Trend following is objective, analytical, and somewhat sedate compared to other portfolio management styles. Imagine CNBC's Joe Kernen saying, "The market continues to be in an uptrend led by technology and transportation stocks," every day for eighteen months. Until one day he comes in and says, "The market uptrend has ended and for now you should consider selling stocks and protecting your account. And now a word from our sponsor."

That approach won't draw in huge numbers of viewers or brokerage advertising dollars, so it will never be given significant airtime. Earnings surprises, GDP revisions, analysts expectations and predictions—all things that are subjective and urgent; that is what the financial media will cover. Those are the types of things that keep viewers and readers interested, which is why Jim Cramer has all those flashing lights and is frequently shouting. Drama equals eyeballs equal victory.

Wall Street, like the financial media, has no proprietary, intrinsic interest in looking out for you. Sure, they would love to see investors do well, but at bottom the mandate remains "grow revenue and earnings by bringing in new assets." That's their job. It is of the utmost importance that they maintain—and grow, if possible—**their market share.** To this end, Wall Street has very deliberately manipulated our expectations and our standards of what constitutes a "desirable outcome."

Most investors use benchmarks to measure the success or failure of their investments. If you asked a room full of investors, "How do you judge your investment advisor?" virtually all of them would answer, "By how he performed relative to the market." So when these investors look at their portfolios, they look first at what the market provided during the same time period, and if they are exceeding that, they consider themselves successful. This is called *relative return investing.* These investors want to perform well on a relative basis.

This seems like a credible way to measure investment performance—that is, in the context of what else was available. And it should be one of the criteria by which you judge performance. If you are trying to match or beat a benchmark that is going up, then even if you just come close, you will be in good shape. The problem comes when the benchmark by which you measure your investment advisor declines by 50 percent.

If your goal is to beat a market that has a 50 percent drop in value, you could accomplish that goal and still lose 40 percent of your capital. We believe there is something fundamentally wrong with that process. If you can accomplish the objective you set out to accomplish and still wind up with 40 percent less money, then what you have is an objective problem. You are trying to do the wrong thing.

Nosce te ipsum: Know thyself. That Latin motto is a critical part of our approach to portfolio management. Our goal is to get our clients what they want and need from their investments. But to get what you want, you have to know yourself, which means being very honest about exactly what you want and exactly what you don't.

When I ask people what they want out of the market, I frequently hear, "I want to beat the market." At first blush that may sound like a reasonable request, and it is certainly one the media has told investors to strive for. It is also a goal that very few people *would* strive for if they had the proper knowledge.

When I look at "the market" returns over the past 50 years, I see there have been three declines of over 48 percent. "Yes," you say, "but the market always recovers." Of course it does. The question is, how long do those recoveries take? The first two recoveries took 90 months and 86 months, respectively, to complete. The most recent decline of 56 percent began in November 2007, bottomed in March of 2009, and didn't fully recover until March of 2013. What if you did in fact "beat the market," and instead of declining 48 percent you only declined 30 percent? And instead of it taking 90 months for you to recover, it took only 80 months? I submit that you had a poor objective to begin with, but you got exactly what you wanted out of the market. You "beat the market," all right. And you lost a lot of money doing it.

The funny thing about this idea of relative performance is how it obscures these bad outcomes. If you ask most investors if they would be comfortable losing 30 or 40 percent of their capital, they would probably be horrified at the thought. Yet, if you contextualize that kind of loss within a market that showed an even greater loss, suddenly that loss becomes more palatable. If you tie your performance to the performance of a market with a huge downside potential, you are essentially signing off on that kind of loss.

Traditional investment firms contextualize performance in this way. It keeps clients invested in a system that isn't actually working for them, and it allows firms to hide among a phalanx of other firms doing exactly the same thing.

Given that, a person can become a very successful investment advisor if he or she does these simple things:

1. Stick close to the market, and if your returns are lackluster, just make sure they aren't too far off market average.
2. Provide customer service. Be friendly, personable, and helpful.
3. Have some degree of financial competence.

In this way, an advisor can build a reliable business (i.e., get clients and keep them). The goal here is not to set yourself apart, but to be no better and no worse than your colleagues. As long as your performance doesn't vary that widely from everyone else's, you will be successful, all through the magic of relative performance!

However, riding the market's coattails can cause problems when the market takes a sudden dip. Clients are bound to be upset when 40 percent or 50 percent of their wealth evaporates because the market entered a bear cycle and nothing was done to protect their capital. Buy-and-hold proponents train investors to accept the benchmarking system for just such occasions. Many investors can be soothed by the idea that it could have been much worse (again, see people bizarrely pleased to "only" lose 40 percent of their capital), but others will inevitably leave their investment advisors.

These investors are frustrated enough to make a change, but the homogenous nature of most investing firms makes it difficult for them to truly alter the way their money is managed. Imagine two investment companies, side-by-side, employing virtually identical investment strategies for clients. In a bull market, when stocks are on the upswing, everyone's assets under management are growing organically, and all the clients are happy. New wealth is being created, and all the companies are getting their share of the new business.

Suddenly, a major bear market cycle interrupts the rise in stocks, and over a period of months prices plummet—down 50 percent. Clients at Firm #1 are furious; they were told to "Just hang in there!" They were told they were diversified, so they were safe. They were told they were buying quality, that the market rewards patience, and all those other bromides—and none of it turned out to be true.

Meanwhile, the clients at Firm #2 are feeling the same way. About half of them decide to stick it out and stay with Firm #2, but the other half decide that they need a change. So where do they go? Well, to distinguished Firm #1, of course. As they walk in the door, whom do they see? The 50 percent of disgruntled clients there who are on their way to Firm #2.

For Wall Street, it's all about market share. In a bull market, everyone keeps their clients, and everyone's assets grow. In a major bear market, firms simply swap clients. There is no true loss for the big firms in terms of market share, and the client gets the comforting illusion that they've made a major change. All this means that there is very little incentive for financial professionals to do anything differently because they are, in many ways, the only game in town. It's as if every team in the NFL worked from the very same playbook.

If every—or nearly every—firm in town is promoting the idea that the market is the best yardstick to measure

... there are good times and bad times to hold any type of asset.

portfolio performance, it begins to seem as though that idea is an immutable fact, rather than a guideline or even an opinion. Consensus often elevates opinions to the status of truths. For example, many investors think of various asset classes as traditionally, even inherently, riskier than others. Similarly, they think of certain investors as fundamentally ill-suited to particular securities because of overgeneralized conventional wisdom. Once again, these beliefs can actually hurt an investor's bottom line.

Some investment firms are what I like to call "asset class and style agnostic." Just as a religious agnostic questions dogma and the existence of absolute truth, these firms don't favor a certain style of investing over another. They do not believe that growth stocks are bad because they are overpriced. Nor do they think that value stocks are the way to go just because they are comparatively inexpensive. As in everything else, you must understand the importance of context: **there are good times and bad times to hold any type of asset**.

Construing certain investments as inherently "bad" or "risky" is part of the strategy for selling investors on the theory of asset allocation. The idea here is that, historically, certain asset classes have correlated to one another in the same way. Gold, for example, has done well in periods of high inflation or periods during which stock prices have done poorly. Traditional firms extrapolate this to suggest that there is a constant inverse relationship between gold and stock prices. The idea is that a portfolio can be balanced in part by putting money into both gold and stocks to "cover" the client in the event of either asset experiencing a big dip.

This is a valid theory, in that the historical correlation between gold and stocks is very low. The typical diversified investment portfolio has a very small allocation to gold and other precious metals. Often the allocation is so small in comparison to the allocation to stocks that the benefit of the gold rally is swallowed up entirely by the huge losses racked up by the stock allocation. It's worth mentioning that, as with other asset classes, there can be long periods during which precious metals prices languish, which makes the obligatory 5 to 10 percent allocation to the asset class a drag on performance much of the time. Wouldn't it be better to make tactical moves in the portfolio, taking into consideration the current state of the markets in stocks, bonds, gold, etc., rather than insisting that one size fits all for most investors and all markets?

Asset allocation and diversification are, in theory, all about lessening the effects of a downturn in any one asset class.

Investors trade a degree of upside potential for the promise that they won't lose as much when the market goes down. There's nothing inherently wrong with this idea. However, asset allocation is virtually the only form of risk management that some firms offer, and like everything else it has its limitations, particularly when put to uses to which it is ill suited. Wall Street's solution to volatility in the market is to spread the money around in every market. If you own everything—growth stocks, bank stocks, emerging market stocks, commodities, and bonds—then you'll never lose it all. This is perhaps more sensible than simply sinking all of your money into Tesla, but it's also a bit of a "brute force" approach.

Instead, I suggest simply paying close attention to the market and what it's telling you. Is the market trending higher? If so, which areas of the market are leading the way? In those leading sectors or industries, which companies are setting the pace? That's a pretty good place to start looking for candidates for the portfolio. Perhaps an investor isn't comfortable owning individual stocks. In that case, allocating capital to leading sectors and avoiding the laggards is a thoughtful and valid approach to investing.

Traditional firms often suggest that this is impossible, but that's simply not true. This approach allows them to shrug off blame when they fail to respond appropriately to a downturn, and it convinces investors that the only way to mitigate risk is to own a bit of everything. It's not unlike buying five television sets with the expectation that some of them will probably be stolen. This may be an effective way to ensure that you can always catch your favorite TV shows, but it might be better to simply buy one television set and then lock your door!

This type of lazy categorization of assets also keeps many investors from fully pursuing all the options available to them. There is a consensus that older people don't need growth stocks—basically that old people can't afford to take risks because they don't have as much time to make up potential losses. Young people, by contrast, should take on lots of risk because they have many years of investing left to them. Clearly, there is wisdom in taking age into consideration when making investment decisions.

Once again, the problem is the over-application of an idea. This rule of thumb isn't without merit, but it shouldn't be a guideline for every situation and every investor. I can't think of a single older person who would not have benefitted from owning Apple stock when it went from $50 per share to $700. There aren't many people too old to enjoy that type of outcome!

Likewise, if you can find a person who is so young and so aggressive that he would have volunteered to hold on to a lot of Enron stock when it went bankrupt, I will eat my hat.

There is no one young enough to accept wholesale, huge levels of downside, and on the other end of the spectrum, no one is so old or so conservative that they need to cut themselves off from any possibility of growth on an upward trend.

Clearly those are extreme examples, but the point is this: There is no one young enough to accept wholesale, huge levels of downside, and on the other end of the spectrum, no one is so old or so conservative that they need to cut themselves off from any possibility of growth on an upward trend.

Once again, the solution is to consider the characteristics of the current market and of the possible investment choices, rather than using a number of flimsy "rules of thumb" that offer a one-size-fits-all solution. The people who benefit from a less rigorous, more generalized approach to investing are the buy-and-hold advisors. They have, unfortunately, convinced many investors that slotting a client's information in a generic set of guidelines is the wisest and safest course of action when, in fact, refusing to evaluate each asset on its own terms only increases the riskiness of the investment. But the good news is that if you take the time to look and ask the right questions, you can find an advisor who will customize your investment portfolio to accomplish your unique objectives within the current market conditions.

CHAPTER FOUR

Who Is Really at Risk?

"The nice part about being a pessimist
is that you are constantly being either
proven right or pleasantly surprised."
—George Will—

NO ONE WANTS to lose money. People with a lot of money *really* don't want to lose money. Taking this into account, it makes sense that risk management would be a big component of every investment strategy. Investors are correctly worried about the market turning on them and consuming a large percentage of their wealth. And yet, many instinctively know that their portfolios are no better protected today than they were in 2008–2009.

What some on Wall Street have done, however, is to redefine risk for most investors, or at least muddy the waters.

Wall Street does everything in its power to reduce risk—risk to themselves, that is.

In 2008, our alarm bells went off. We are constantly monitoring all markets for certain indicators that have historically preceded significant tops, both for individual stocks and for the market in general. At that time our research was telling us that the uptrend we had enjoyed since 2003 was over. We had no idea what was going to happen in the future—no one does—but we did know that, according to our observations about price and volume activity in the market, the current trend was ending.

Watching trends is useful only if you actually act in accordance with your conclusions, which we did. We got out of stocks, and we did it several weeks before Lehman Brothers imploded—several weeks before the end of the financial world as we knew it.

Our system worked. We saw the indicators and did what we said we would do in that situation—and it saved our clients (and us) a lot of money. Our accounts weren't entirely immune, and we did suffer losses in that cycle. But getting out when we did (August of 2008) mitigated the damage. We had a system of objective measurements that were linked to specific actions. Following through on previously established rules allowed us to mute the impact of a major crisis.

The funny thing was … few people seemed to see it that way. I've been in the money management business for twenty years, and I have friends and colleagues from all over the country and in all corners of the financial sector. When I talked to them during this time, when the market was getting hammered and so many people were losing so much, I was often met with confusion and skepticism.

"We're out of stocks," I said.

They looked at me blankly. "What do you mean? Like … you don't have much in stocks?"

"No, I mean we're out. We have no exposure to stocks."

Without exception, every one of those people would follow up with something to the effect of, "Boy, that's risky." Remember, we were entirely in cash, we had no exposure to stocks, and the market was experiencing the worst collapse since 1929, and the universal response was that *our* choices were the risky ones!

What does Wall Street really mean when it talks about risk? Certainly not what most investors think of when they imagine risk. For one thing, traditional firms strongly privilege "opportunity risk," which is the risk you take by not participating in a given investment. This is the risk that if you don't buy something for $100 today, it could leap up to $200 tomorrow and you would miss out entirely. It's also the risk you take by choosing one investment over another.

When I think of opportunity risk, I think of my wife. On the day I met her, when I first noticed her and became interested, I was faced with a couple of different types of risk. If I approached her right then and asked her out, I was running the risk that she would laugh me out of the place. I was risking rejection, which would have ruined my day. On the other hand, if I didn't speak to her, I risked losing an opportunity. In this case, it was the opportunity to get to know my future wife and the mother of my children.

Let's discuss several types of risk. First, there's *absolute risk*. This is the money that can be lost in an investment. The amount of money you are willing to lose on an investment is your absolute risk.

But there's also something called *relative performance risk*. Relative performance risk is exactly what it sounds like—it's the risk of underperforming a benchmark or your competitors. In other words, it's the risk that although the market goes up, you don't fully participate in it.

As we've discussed before, the worst thing a buy-and-hold advisor can do is fall out of lockstep with the competition. They value conformity, even if it means taking a nosedive along with everyone else.

For this type of company, nothing looks worse than sitting out during a spike in the market. It is actually preferable for them to have their clients 100 percent invested in the market and have the market drop 30 percent than to be caught holding cash when the market goes up 15 percent. They prioritize any upside potential over the most precipitous drop.

What's worse is that they've nurtured this way of thinking

in their clients. They present risks to the advisor (the risk of looking bad, the risk of falling behind) as risk to the investor, and they prey upon the human fear of being an outlier. No one wants to be left behind; no one wants to miss out on something.

The dilemma is this: How do you balance the risk of losing money with the risk of underperforming if the markets are rising? There are times when a buy-and-hold approach works better than any sort of tactical investing, and these periods can be frustrating for tactical investors (especially new ones) who want their investment accounts to go up as much as the market does.

When evaluating an investment strategy over a ten-year time frame, it's easy to focus on the total returns and overlook the shorter time periods that make up the total. An advisor is likely to show a strategy that works well over a period of five to ten years but, because the strategy isn't geared toward "beating the market," an investor can be surprised by poor returns during some shorter time period.

An example may help here. You are considering a tactical strategy that has compounded capital at 15 percent a year over ten years, with a maximum peak-to-trough decline of 20 percent.

Year 1 +16.8%	Year 5 +40%	Year 8 +11.6%
Year 2 +15.6%	Year 6 +13.9%	Year 9 +23%
Year 3 +21.5%	Year 7 +6.8%	Year 10 +11.5%
Year 4 -0.5%		

You like that the strategy only lost money in one year, and even then it was less than 1 percent. What can't be seen in this presentation is the 120 rolling twelve-month time frames (ten years times twelve months). An investor isn't likely to invest on the very first day of a calendar year. If the maximum decline of 20 percent began midway through year and lasted for six months, any investor who invested in June or July was down around 20 percent by the year's end. If in year five the bulk of the returns came in the second half of the year, it's conceivable that, two years in, the investor is down 20 percent, even though the investment strategy's annual returns show now annual loss greater than 1%.

How did this happen? What doesn't show up in the calendar year returns is that, midway through year three, the strategy was up 50 percent on a year-to-date basis. Looking at the calendar year return of 21.5 percent obscures the huge run-up in the first half of the year and the 20 percent decline in the second half. As we've discussed, facts can be presented in a way that are at once true and misleading.

Wall Street brokers and advisors are required by regulatory bodies to "know the customer" and to recommend investments that are "suitable." If Wall Street requires brokers and advisors to know the customer, you have a duty to know yourself. If the scenario above is more than you can stand, you'd better have some of your investment capital allocated to strategies that go up when the market goes up.

A solution to this conundrum is to allocate capital to both absolute and relative return strategies. If you don't structure your investments in a way that fits your temperament, the likelihood is high that you will make a bad decision when you are stressed by your investment getting crushed in a market decline or by sitting out a big move up.

On a personal note, Joy and I were married in her hometown of Lake Village, Arkansas, one year after we met. The date was set for October 8, 1994. October is a beautiful month, especially in the South, where in contrast to the 100-degree August temperatures, October welcomes you with a cool breeze. That was the very reason we picked that day—the weather is almost always perfect in early October.

For years my wife had dreamed of having her wedding in the little church a few blocks from where she grew up. She knew the ceremony would be followed by a reception at her childhood home, situated picturesquely on beautiful Lake Chicot. The turn-of-the-century house she lived in has a lovely front yard, which she imagined would serve as the dance floor. There, on the soft grass, she and her new husband (me) would dance to "At Last" as the guests looked on, their eyes dewy with hope at the promise of young love.

Things didn't quite go as planned.

One of the worst rainstorms Arkansas has ever seen hit that very October day, just as we were leaving the church. The fact that rain was statistically unlikely in October certainly

Wall Street may have a reputation to lose if they don't catch every single upward trend, but investors have real money to lose if they aren't careful.

didn't assuage the feelings of the bride—or her mother, who had spent months collaborating closely with Joy, planning every little detail. It didn't matter to either of them that almost every other October day is perfect, because the only day that mattered, October 8, 1994, was a washout. The fact that they had *planned* it so perfectly, doing everything possible to ensure a beautiful day, was like pouring salt into the wound.

So it is for investors who do as the experts instruct. The fact that they had followed expert advice in relying on the long-term returns of the market, asset allocation, and diversification was little consolation to those who retired in 2007 with unprotected exposure to stocks. What happens "on average" doesn't matter nearly as much as what *actually* happens.

It does investors no favors to constantly chase the performance of the market or some other benchmark. Wall Street may have a reputation to lose if they don't catch every single upward trend, but investors have real money to lose if they aren't careful. Whom would you rather protect?

CHAPTER FIVE

Lose Your Losers ...
And Let Your Winners Run

"Taking small losses is part of the game.
Taking large losses can take you out of the game."
—Doug Kass—

THERE IS AN old adage about playing bridge: "Lose your losers."
It cautions players against running from losing cards, hoping
to turn them into winning tricks late in the game. That strategy almost never works, and can actually turn winning cards
(cards that should win a trick) into losers. If this happens, the
player risks losing control of the game.

"Lose your losers" is really a caution against allowing
emotion to overpower good judgment. And it's not just
valuable advice for bridge—it translates surprisingly well to
the investment world. Much like a deck of cards, the market

Human beings are prone to biases that inhibit our ability to make good decisions.

does not care what you want, and it has no particular desire to see you succeed.

Much has been written in the last ten years about human bias and the sometimes strange ways our brains actually undermine our efforts to serve our own best interests. The field of behavioral finance is in its infancy, but anyone who has observed investor behavior for any length of time already has a pretty good idea of the kinds of biases that can harm an otherwise savvy investor. Investing is chockfull of people who draw causal lines between events without data or scientific proof. Maybe they do it out of excitement, or perhaps they do it out of fear. Either way, these people are slaves to their emotions, and as soon as emotions get involved, things are apt to go haywire.

Human beings are prone to biases that inhibit our ability to make good decisions. Here are just a few:

- **Loss Aversion**: The tendency for people to have a strong preference for avoiding losses over acquiring gains. Some studies suggest that losses are twice as psychologically powerful as gains.

- **Disposition Effect**: The tendency of investors to sell shares whose price has increased, while keeping assets that have dropped in value.
- **Outcome Bias**: The tendency to judge a decision by its outcome rather than by the quality of the decision at the time it was made.
- **Bandwagon Bias**: Believing something primarily because many others believe it.
- **The Law of Small Numbers Bias**: Drawing unjustified conclusions from too little information.
- **Hindsight Bias**: The belief that some past event was predictable when in reality it wasn't.
- **Confirmation Bias**: The tendency to seek out information that confirms an existing belief.

Any one of these biases can sink a person if it interferes at a critical moment.

Biases are fundamentally human, and most of us have these and other biases at work in us much of the time. We at Woodbridge know we aren't free from bias, and we don't pretend to be. Instead, we've built into our portfolio management systems mechanisms for identifying and accounting for these biases. We've worked to mitigate the negative impact biases have on all our portfolio management systems.

We endeavor to avoid emotion-based decision-making. To that end, we work with a number of rules and predetermined guidelines. When we make an investment, we have a clear plan of action for how to proceed if it begins to perform poorly. In this way, we head off loss before it becomes meaningful to the portfolio.

We consider ourselves to be market historians. We are students of the market, and we pay close attention to what the market tells us about winners and losers. We start with a simple question: Are there characteristics, quantifiable conditions, fundamental data, that are present in past winners? Are these conditions common among the big stock-market winners of the past?

Our research indicates that **not only were there common characteristics present among many of history's biggest winners, but these conditions were present *before* the stock became a big winner**. It's not very useful to know about commonalities, after all, if none of them are predictors. We have overwhelmingly found that certain things about companies can be known publicly, and often those things can predict a big winner.

Say there are 3,000 growth stocks and you have identified ten major qualities or characteristics that big winners had before they became big winners (return on equity, a certain earnings growth, revenue growth, etc.). With this information, you can winnow those 3,000 stocks down to a more manageable number.

Now, this doesn't mean that you are going to have all winners on your hands—far from it. Of that number, a fairly small number may be big winners, and maybe one of those will turn out to be a Google. But success is possible even if you don't pinpoint *any* of the huge breakout stars.

We have shrunk our universe considerably, and we know that the percentage of winners in our universe will be larger than the percentage of winners in the population of stocks at large, but we still need to do more to determine which companies are more likely than others to pull ahead of the pack.

This is where the price trend comes in. We believe that **price is the most telling piece of public information we can have about a company.** One important element in our portfolio management systems is that the stock being considered for purchase must already be exhibiting positive price

> **... price is the most telling piece of public information we can have about a company.**

performance. If a stock has all the qualities of a big winner but is in a downtrend, then we'd rather wait it out on the sidelines or invest in something else. There is just no good reason to rush to invest money in something that is headed in the wrong direction.

At all times, we defer to the stock price trend. Price is the canary in the coalmine—it tells us that something is wrong with a stock long before the problem is common knowledge. Just as we have identified certain characteristics as being associated with winning stocks, there are specific behaviors (of which a decline in price trend is MOST important) that often indicate a company is in trouble.

It is vitally important when selecting companies with which to build a portfolio that you have a plan for elimi- . nating losers before they can do much damage. Even if you are stacking the deck in your favor by selecting stocks with important predictors, you still have to provide for the possibility—no, the *probability*—that you are sometimes going to be wrong. In fact, we start with the idea that we are going to be wrong about some of the stocks we select for the portfolio. Thankfully, the stock price trend usually provides us with the information we need to determine whether the investment is in trouble. All we have to do is pay attention.

As it turns out, this is much more difficult than it at first appears to be. We wouldn't need the "lose your losers" adage if people didn't tend to hold on to useless cards that only weaken their hand. There is a powerful emotional component to investing, and too often people allow their feelings to override their judgment and inhibit their own ability to be effective investors.

This is not to say that we must scrub all bias from our portfolio. If, for example, you don't want to own tobacco, or casino or oil stocks, that's a completely reasonable restriction and it's your individual decision to make. You just eliminate those industries from the pool of eligible investments.

The unexamined bias is more dangerous. Believing, for example, that tech stocks are inherently risky, or that utility stocks are safe and can't hurt you, can dampen returns and even increase risk. It's very easy to convince ourselves that we know a lot more than we actually do.

As I mentioned previously, some trends last decades. Trends can go on for so long that they convince us that certain conditions are absolutes, when in fact they are still only temporary. Sometimes it only takes a few years to condition us to a certain "reality," especially if it's a reality we like. Everyone wants to believe they are smart and effective. Why would we want to believe the opposite?

That's why people who have made a lot of money in the real estate sector often imagine that they know all there is to know about real estate investments. They believe they have expertise, and if they are investing during an uptrend of several years, their belief will be reinforced. The longer someone is on an upward trend, the more powerfully they believe that they have a special understanding of the sector in which they are investing. All of this is well and good … until it isn't.

The dynamics of markets invariably change. Hard and fast notions like "utility stocks are safe" simply don't hold true over a sufficiently long period of time. When the stocks in a sector begin to drop in price—when what was the low-end valuation becomes the high-end valuation—we aren't alerted to the change by the company or by industry analysts. The company doesn't say, "Our earnings multiple, which used to trade at a high of 25 times forward earning expectations, now ranges from a low of 5 to a high of 12." Even company insiders don't know that a sea change has taken place, so it's impossible for an investor or an advisor to discern the shift. The unchecked belief that the range should be 10 on the low side and 25 on the high side based on how the stock traded for many years is a costly one if the range has fundamentally changed. Those biases can keep investors buried deep in a stock or sector long after its time has come and gone, because when their vision of how the stock should perform conflicts with reality, they choose their vision.

Take the case of WorldCom, a telecom juggernaut that nevertheless famously filed for bankruptcy in 2002. I am from Mississippi, and WorldCom was a Mississippi company that inspired a great deal of local pride. The company provided thousands of people with good, high-paying jobs.

These employees were rewarded with stock options that sky-rocketed in value as the company grew. There were more than a few stories of everyday people becoming very wealthy as a result of their affiliation with WorldCom. Throughout the nineties, WorldCom was one of the best-performing public companies, dwarfing the returns of companies like Apple. It seemed as if it would never end.

The problem was that once WorldCom began to clearly decline, those feelings of pride and attendant goodwill didn't decline at the same rate the stock price did. People still liked WorldCom; they wanted to believe it could bounce back. Many people also felt a personal connection to the company. For any number of reasons, many stockholders decided to ignore the information that the stock price trend was giving them and instead hoped for a recovery. People believed in the company. But why would anyone "believe" in a company?

Let's take another look at General Electric. As the stock was topping out at $60 in the spring of 2000, many analysts had "Buy" or "Strong Buy" ratings on the company stock. Most had a "target price" of $100 or more. How could so many smart people on Wall Street get it so wrong? Let's first look at the mechanics of how these so-called "target" prices get set.

Primarily, two factors determine the market price of every profitable company: earnings and price-to-earnings multiple. While we know that earnings are routinely restated by public companies, let's assume for now that if a company says they made $1.00 a share, they really did make it.

GE made $1.27 a share in 2000. The high was $60, which made the price-to-earnings multiple 47 (60/1.27=47). The earnings multiple is the value the market places on a future income stream; it can and does fluctuate wildly. GE traded as low as $41 in 2000, making the low price-to-earnings multiple 32.

In general, a Wall Street analyst will estimate future earnings assuming past-earnings growth rates accelerate. So the analyst may believe that by 2007, General Electric's earnings per share will be $2.10 and the earnings multiple will expand by 25 percent to 58, yielding a target price of $121.80. Let's see what actually happened.

In 2007, General Electric earned $2.17 a share (better than our fictional estimate), and yet the high for the stock was $42, or 19x earnings. Not only do analysts need to get the earnings estimate right (they frequently do not), they also have to correctly forecast the value (earnings multiple) the market is going to give to the future earnings. And who can blame them for not getting it right—it's impossible to predict the future!

What if I told you I knew company ABC was going to double its earnings over the next five years and you should put every dime you could find into the stock? Furthermore, if you held the stock for five years, I guaranteed 100 percent of your investment if I ended up being wrong about the company and it didn't double its earnings. Now assume that I can make good on the guarantee and there's no risk that I won't. Would you take that deal?

Let's say you buy $1 million worth of the stock and hold it for five years, at which time you see that your investment is worth $100,000. Yikes. "No problem," you think, and come knocking on my door for a full refund—which I promptly deny. Under what possible scenario could I legitimately refuse to make good on the guarantee? If ABC Company *did* double its earnings, but the stock got crushed anyway, your request to be made whole is invalid. The point is that a company's earnings can go up and its share price can still go down. Your investment was insured in one way, but you didn't have the equivalent of flood insurance!

The fact of the matter is, once you take a position in a stock or ETF, there are only three things that can happen, and two of them aren't good. Furthermore, we as investors have no control over which of the three actually happens.

Here are the possibilities:

1. It goes up. Great! This is exactly the outcome you want.
2. It goes down. Not great, this is exactly what you are trying to avoid.
3. It does nothing. Also not great. A flat stock is just taking up space in your portfolio.

"Imagine you have $25 in your pocket; would you take that $25 out of your pocket and invest it in this stock? If not, you should probably sell it."

Inevitably one of these three things will happen, and we have absolutely no say in the matter. That may seem like an obvious point, but the only reason people wind up owning hundreds of thousands of shares of a WorldCom or an Enron when they go bankrupt—the only reason people lose 100 percent of an investment like that—is because they are unwilling to sell it. They have a conviction that the company or the industry will rally, and they trust this emotion over objective evidence to the contrary.

This is where bias can really harm an investor. If he believes he has some specialized knowledge about a company because he is familiar with it or with the industry, then he believes he knows more than the market. It is this blind conviction that causes him to "stay the course" even as the train goes off the rails. When making the decision to hold or sell a stock in which you have a loss, consider whether you would invest in it *today* if you didn't currently own it. A good friend puts it this way: "Imagine you have $25 in your pocket; would you take that $25 out of your pocket and invest it in this stock? If not, you should probably sell it."

In contrast, we know we don't have any knowledge that the market hasn't given us. We know that the power and influence lie elsewhere. Coca-Cola does not ask us for advice about a new line of soft drinks or how to deploy the cash on their balance sheet. All of those things are happening on a different level, and we cannot affect those decisions. The only thing we can control after we enter a position is when we exit. Period. Exclamation point!

So, once we do take a position in a stock, our main job becomes one of observation. The stock will perform how it performs—it's either going to be a winner, a loser, or a laggard. And the only thing we can control is how we respond to that performance. We initiate the pre-existing protocol and then manage the trade based on what type of performer it turns out to be. If the stock begins to show signs of being a loser, we have a pre-defined point at which we will exit the trade, no questions asked. That point is unique to every stock—for example, if we buy a stock at $50, we may decide to sell it if it hits $45.

This practice doesn't mean you suddenly have a bias against whatever stock you have eliminated. If you notice that telecom stocks are exhibiting symptoms of a downturn, you get rid of telecom stocks promptly, but that doesn't mean you can't re-invest in telecom stocks when they start showing desirable characteristics a few years or even months down the road. The great thing about using objective evidence to make decisions is that it gives you considerably more flexibility. There are no "bad" assets, just ones that are currently performing poorly. As an investor, you are not hemmed in by stereotypes about safety and risk that don't necessarily hold true.

This is the way to keep and grow wealth. You continue to own investments that are presently improving the condition of your portfolio, and you systematically eliminate those that are not. This goes for whole asset classes as well as for individual stocks.

Now how do we manage the winning trade? The previous rules are what we call "loser rules," and they are largely designed to protect our (client) principal. They reduce the negative impact of any given loser. The "winner rules" are designed to maximize the total return contribution that a stock can provide to the portfolio.

We never know how a stock is going to perform after we buy it. Sometimes we buy a stock with all the characteristics we are looking for just as it's beginning a really nice move.

Let me show you how this might work. First, a few assumptions:

1. $1,000,000 investment account
2. 5% position taken in a stock trading at $40 a share (1250 shares)
3. .5% of account equity risked on the trade ($5,000)
4. Stop loss of $36 (when to sell a loser)
5. Trailing stop is a 20% decline from the highest close (when to sell a winner)

You now own 1250 shares of a stock that you bought at $40 a share. If the stock trades below $36 you are going to sell it, keeping your losses at $5000 or less. If the stock begins to go up, you want to let it go as much as possible before selling it so you decide that if it declines by 20% from the high (after you buy it) you will use this as your exit. The first thing I notice about this scenario is that you have capped your losses at $5000 but you've left your upside uncapped (you know only that you won't let it decline by more than 20% from the high trade after you own it; you have no idea how high that may be). So, how *could* this work out?

During the week of October 1, 2010, you take a position in Apple at about $40 a share. If you employed the rules above you would have exited Apple at about $80 during the week of 11/9/2012. The profit on the trade was $50,000 and you added 5% to the value of your account…by risking .5% of the value of your account. You risked $5000 and made $50,000. That's a good risk reward. Now before you say I'm "cherry picking" Apple, let me assure you that there are an almost infinite number of trades that I could have picked from, many that have a far more impressive result than this example. And, Apple very well may go much, much higher in the future (who knows), but what we are illustrating is a way to manage a winning trade as it unfolds in real time.

Do you see how employing a strategy that measures risk in this way can produce nice returns with palatable risk to your principal?

The significant point is that our focus here is on maximizing profits. This is in contrast to positions that go against us early on, when we are laser-focused on limiting the damage they can do. Managing a winning trade is more complicated than managing a losing or lagging trade. To a great degree the condition of the overall market or sector in which the stock trades can affect how it's managed. In general, staying with a winning position is advisable, as long as the basic nature of the stock doesn't change.

When we lose our losers and laggards, we free up capital that we can then re-allocate into other positions that could become winners. One of the many ways that Wall Street sells its universal "buy-and-hold" model is to say that they "buy quality companies and hold them until the fundamentals change." This naturally raises the question, "How do you know when the fundamentals of a company have changed?"

Perhaps it's when the earnings fall or don't grow at the expected rate? Or when revenues begin to stagnate, or the competition begins grabbing market share? Nearly 100 percent of the time we find out what fundamental problems the company was having when the stock falls from $75 to $15. Inevitably, the price trend will tell you the true story. The problem with the "buy quality and hold it for the long term" idea is that if you do so in the face of a falling price trend, you end up going down with a ship instead of exiting it when it was merely taking on water. As long as you believe that the fundamentals are unchanged, you will look for information that confirms this belief. And once you know exactly what's wrong with the fundamentals, it's often too late to change the outcome for yourself and your portfolio.

Many people believe that utility stocks are inherently stable while technology stocks are inherently risky. But a careful examination of the evidence proves this to be false. In

The problem with the "buy quality and hold it for the long term" idea is that if you do so in the face of a falling price trend, you end up going down with a ship instead of exiting it when it was merely taking on water.

the last cyclical bear market, Microsoft fell 59 percent, while Entergy, a public utility, fell 53 percent. Since then Microsoft has made up the entire loss, while Entergy remains 48 percent below its 2007 high.

It's obvious that neither of these is a good outcome, but it's certainly worth noting that you simply can't make sweeping generalizations about sectors or the markets in which they trade. On the upside, some of these companies can post staggering returns. A stock may go from $50 to $300. Investing in that doesn't seem like a very risky choice to me. And yet, an obvious success like a stock increasing six times in value can actually be used to justify a bias against tech stocks.

Wall Street often views upside volatility the very same way it views downside volatility. If a stock goes from $100 to $200, it has the exact same level of volatility as a stock that goes from $100 to $50. Stock A ($100 to $200) and Stock B ($100 to $50) have the exact same standard deviation, but I think we all know which one we would rather have in our portfolio!

This is yet another case of Wall Street applying generalizations across the board and ignoring context. Upside volatility is not the same as downside volatility, and it should not be treated in the same way. However, if you are viewing anything through the prism of a pre-established opinion, even the positive attributes of a stock or industry can be turned into negatives. Unfortunately, this often means missing out on a lot of opportunities for growth.

Trend analysis is not perfect, but it is also not biased or rooted in emotion. Trend analysis is built around objective evidence, and it starts with an admission of just how little we really know. If we accept that our knowledge is limited, we can also accept the importance of the information we do have, instead of insisting that we somehow "know better."

Pride, ego, and emotion will absolutely lie to you every time. The numbers never will.

CHAPTER SIX

Over-Diversification Is Overrated

"The four most expensive words in the English
language are, 'This time it's different.'"
—Sir John Templeton—

AT ITS HEART, the diversification strategy of portfolio management can be boiled down to one simple aphorism: don't put
all your eggs in one basket. This advice stands the test of
time because it's an important element of a solid strategy. In
finance, the thinking goes, "If you keep some of your wealth
in a variety of asset types, you will never lose everything."
(Now *that's* an inspired objective!) If stocks are performing
poorly, perhaps your bonds may smooth out the ride. And
if bonds are making a lackluster showing, surely your stocks
will turn enough profit to even things out. The idea is that

the diversity of your portfolio is your safety net—and there is some truth to it.

However, there are limitations to diversification in many cases, especially when it serves as the primary risk management tool. For instance, over-diversification in an up market is almost always going to hurt returns. If the market goes up 30 percent and you only have 30 percent of your money in stocks and the rest in bonds, then you are going to have a much smaller return than if you were more heavily weighted in stocks.

Diversification is supposed to protect the investor against a down market. When diversification works, it is because the portfolio is full of assets that have low correlations to one another—meaning the performance of one asset is not typically tied to the other asset classes in the portfolio. All this can go out the window, though, given a big enough market downturn. And when certain situations come along, correlations can "flip." What was previously non-correlated can become highly correlated. What does this mean for a carefully assembled portfolio filled with products that aren't supposed to be correlated with one another? It can mean plummeting values across the board—exactly what most investors try to avoid.

A word about inflation and its impact on financial assets: Ed Easterling with Crestmont Research has written two books and developed a web-based series of classes on—among other things—the effect of the inflation rate on financial assets. Investors who want an in-depth discussion of these and other concepts can look to Crestmont Research for those resources. For the sake of this discussion I'm going to ask the reader to agree with Easterling (and almost all financial and economic experts) that a rising inflation rate is bad for financial asset (stock and bond) prices.

Most of us experienced the last two cyclical bear markets in real time. We personally lost money and endured the emotional trauma of those losses. During the tech bubble bust (2000–2002) bonds did very well, even as stock prices plummeted. Likewise, during the financial crisis there was a "flight to quality" into bonds as the stock market melted down. In each of these declines a balanced portfolio of *stocks and bonds* performed much better than a portfolio heavily concentrated only in stocks. In an inflationary bear market, bonds will not offer the same refuge. Few investors have experienced an inflationary bear market firsthand. During an inflationary bear market, both stock and bond prices will decline.

Conventional wisdom says that bonds are good diversifiers of stocks. On a daily or monthly basis, stock and bond prices can and do move in different directions, which means that the previous statement is true, in a sense. But a closer look reveals that during "time periods that are relevant to investors," as Ed Easterling puts it, stock and bond prices are more highly correlated. Easterling points out that during decades (a far more relevant time period to investors than days or months) in which the inflation rate is rising or declining, stocks and bonds tend to move in tandem. As the inflation rate increased during the 1970s, bond returns (those with longer maturities) were even worse than stock market returns. Conversely, in periods during which inflation is decreasing, like the 1980s and 1990s, stock and bond prices tend to rise.

The point here is that, once again, Wall Street has misapplied a principle. In this case, they have overlooked the fact that while stock and bond prices do move somewhat independently of one another in the short term (days and months), over longer and more relevant time periods to investors, they tend to be more highly correlated. This is important because many investors own a balanced portfolio of stocks and bonds (due to lessons learned in the last two cyclical bear markets) that they believe will protect them in all bear markets. When (not *if*) inflation begins to rise, these investors will be surprised to see that their bonds, which they had regarded as the "safe" part of their investment portfolios, might very well be the worst performers of all the investments they own.

Remember, the stock market has averaged 10 percent a year since the mid 1920s. Some advisors (and conventional wisdom) use this statistic to encourage investors to stay invested in the market at all times. As we've discussed, this statistic considers a ninety-year period of time; unless you have a time frame consistent with the period of time over which that average return was generated, it is meaningless to you.

Now, rather than using a statistic based on too much time (ninety years) to get investors to buy and hold investments even during bear markets, Wall Street uses a statistic based on *too little* time (days and months) to give investors the impression that a balanced portfolio of stocks and bonds will protect them in all bad markets.

It is fascinating that a ninety-year average annual return is inappropriately used to get investors to stay invested during all market conditions, and that the low correlation between stocks and bonds over a very short period of time is used to support the idea that a 60/40 stock and bond portfolio will provide the investor needed risk and return diversification.

During deflation, however, bonds will generate positive returns, while stock prices will suffer terrible performance. Although deflation occurs far less frequently than inflation, it certainly could crop up sometime in the future.

Too often, a firm will set up a hard and fast portfolio split, and *refuse* to deviate from it, no matter how the assets in question are actually performing.

For example, imagine you are doing your quarterly rebalancing, and for the sake of simplicity, let's say you have a diversity strategy of keeping 50 percent of your money in stocks and 50 percent in bonds. Let's say you have $1 million in stocks and $1 million in bonds. When you check your portfolio, you see that stocks are up 10 percent and bonds are flat. Because of your stock performance, you now have an additional $100,000 to reinvest. With your diversity plan in place, there's only one thing to do: you split it, putting $50,000 in stocks and $50,000 in bonds. Your 50/50 split is maintained. In the next quarter, when you return to rebalance the portfolio, you find that stocks are up an additional 10 percent and bonds are now down 10 percent. Once again, you recalibrate by taking half the profits from the gains in your stock portfolio and adding it to the bond portfolio.

Are you seeing how this sort of strategy can hurt you in the long run? It's the exact opposite of "losing your losers" and letting your winners run. Instead, you are selling the assets that are working for you and putting that money back into assets that are performing poorly. By doing this, you rob yourself of compounding returns. Ironically, because stocks and bonds tend to be non-correlated in the short term, the investor is denied even that benefit by employing such a strategy. In other words, it is only in the short term that bonds are good diversifiers of stocks, and so to trim the position that is working in favor of the other defeats the very purpose of the diversity, especially when you consider that on a longer-term basis stocks and bonds can be highly correlated.

I'll give you an example of a strategy we use that is intended to give our clients the benefit of diversification and the power of investing in the right areas of the market. Research shows that positive short-term price momentum is predictive of future short-term performance. The research suggests those asset classes that have performed well in the recent past are statistically likely to perform well in the near future.[1] This is in direct contrast to research indicating long-term positive performance can be predictive of poor performance in the future.

With this system, we start with an investment universe that represents most of the global market and includes stocks, bonds, and commodities. In this system we use ETFs, but you could use mutual funds or even futures for that matter. We rank each member of the universe from top to bottom using a simple calculation based on several months of past performance data. The purpose of this ranking is to determine which members of the universe have performed the best over the look-back period. We then invest in the top two or three members of the universe (depending on the objective) and hold them for the next three months. Pretty simple, right? This leads us into the most productive areas of the global market, relative to the rest of the universe.

---

1 Narasimhan Jegadeesh and Sheridan Titman, "Momentum," The National Bureau of Economic Research, August 29, 2011.

We know from experience, however, that there are times when even the best relative performers don't make for very good investments. To account for that reality we've inserted an element we call a "safety filter" that prevents the portfolio from investing in any instrument trading below an intermediate-term moving average (tracking the average price for the security over the look-back period allows us to see if the ETF is trending higher or lower). So if the top members of the universe, according to the performance ranking, are themselves trending lower, the portfolio is forced out of that market and into cash or short-term treasuries.

This leads us into a portfolio of investments that are diverse by their nature (ETFs or Funds) and statistically likely to perform better than other alternatives. So, under the right circumstances, even sixty-five-year-old Aunt Mary can be invested in emerging markets. Likewise, when risk is higher, twenty-five-year-old Cousin Eddie is invested in short-term treasuries. In other words, we let the market be our guide, rather than being stuck in a rigid asset allocation model.

Not only does this make sense intuitively, but this strategy and others like it can dramatically improve performance and reduce drawdown when compared to a buy-and-hold approach. Combining a strategy like this with several other strategies that consider other performance and drawdown characteristics provides real diversification. Do you see how applying these principles to your portfolio could improve the quality of your investment experience, and by extension, the quality of your life? Why not employ diversification strategically rather than simply owning everything and keeping your fingers crossed, hoping that you "won't lose everything"?

Nevertheless, that is what Wall Street would have you do, all in the name of "safety." This "Buy, Hold, and Hope" concept asks us to set aside our capacity for reason. In no other area of our lives would we ever ignore relevant information and forge ahead in defiance of reality.

Our experience has led us to reject diversification as a "magic bullet" approach. Instead of just spreading money around widely with the hope that the sheer breadth of your portfolio will save you, we prefer to invest our clients' money more precisely and deliberately. Why invest in everything to be "safe" when you can instead simply invest in the areas of the market that are exhibiting the strongest characteristics?

Our company practices what is called "tactical allocation." This means, essentially, that we identify those asset classes that are performing well and funnel capital into them. All this is accomplished within the pre-defined strategic allocation set by the client in consultation with us. A client with a balanced portfolio objective may set maximum and minimum exposures to an asset class. In this case, for example, the equity allocation may range from a maximum of 60 percent to a minimum of 10 percent. So, in the best conditions, the account may have 60 percent exposure to stocks, and even in the very worst conditions an allocation of 10 percent must be maintained.

We recognize the very basic truth that sometimes stocks do poorly and sometimes bonds do well. Instead of ignoring the reality of what these asset classes are doing, we capitalize on it. Maintaining a well-positioned portfolio requires you to do more than just spread the money around equally. A portfolio should be, above all else, effective. If it's packed full of dead weight products simply for the purpose of parity, then it loses its usefulness.

Buying a stock, bond, mutual fund, or any other type of financial product is in many ways like entering a relationship. We invest ourselves to some degree and tie our fates to these assets. The fundamental difference is that Wall Street demands we accept behaviors in these "relationships" that we would never accept from the people in our lives.

Imagine you go out on a first date. She shows up late, guzzles a bottle of Thunderbird, and gets into a fight with the waiter. Then, on the way home, she vomits in your car. How would you feel about a second date? Because that is exactly what Wall Street expects you to do with their type of asset allocation. No matter how many red flags there are or how much it hurts, you stick with it because you are committed to the allocation. It's as if, after that terrible date, you'd said to yourself, "Well, she's completely awful, but she's blond, green-eyed, and five-foot-eight, so I guess I should marry her."

Perhaps the greatest flaw of the diversification strategy is the way it lulls investors into a false sense of security. A feeling of security is surprisingly powerful. When investors feel safe and comfortable, it's very easy for them to blindly trust whoever is selling them that safety. It's very easy for them to slack the reins on their portfolio and simply let the investment firm they've chosen handle their asset allocation.

As we said before, however, there are no crystal balls that perfectly predict the future. Wall Street implies that their diversity strategy will protect you from market fluctuations, all while maintaining plausible deniability. Then, when a 40 percent decline in the market happens and your assets are suddenly taking huge hits, that's when the buy-and-hold advisor will look at you and say, "Hey, who could have possibly predicted this?"

Cash is a valid asset class, and it should play a role in portfolio management. The inability or unwillingness to reduce exposure to the market in certain circumstances is to investing what a refusal to use the brake is to driving.

The fact is that disasters happen, and in investing they happen with some regularity. If your "safe" strategy counts on you just swallowing any losses that result from relatively frequent disasters, then it's not really all that safe, is it?

We make no claim to be able to predict the future, but we do know that certain indicators can appear before a big decline in the market. Through statistical analysis and trend following, we attempt to reduce risk to the investor by reducing or eliminating their exposure to asset classes that are showing pre-established markers of big impending problems.

In the summer of 2001, Joy and I found out we were going to have our second child. During her first visit to the OB/GYN, the doctor found a small lump in her breast. He examined it, quickly determined it was a cyst, and assured her it was nothing to be concerned about. The lump continued to grow, and on each subsequent visit we would raise the issue; and his response was always the same: "Nothing to worry about. No big deal." He didn't order a mammogram and continued to insist that it was fibrocystic disease.

Months went by, and Joy was seven months pregnant when, for some reason, I blurted out at a family dinner, "Joy has a lump in her breast and it's growing." Within two weeks, a biopsy was performed and Joy was diagnosed with cancer. She has since made a full recovery, but that recovery was very much in doubt for the twelve months following the diagnosis.

When I told the OB/GYN he had missed the diagnosis, he said to me, "The chance that was breast cancer was 1 in 10,000." And I was supposed to just accept that? The statistical improbability of an outcome is of zero value to the 1 in

10,000. If my daughter Grace had 10,000 mothers and I had 10,000 wives, that might have been some consolation, but as it stood we each had just the one. To Joy, there was no consolation.

The point here is that there are always signs before something goes wrong. Just as a doctor shouldn't ignore a patient's symptoms, we shouldn't overlook indications that an investment may be in trouble. These indications are the signposts we use to protect ourselves.

Too often, though, I see a kind of fiscal "Stockholm Syndrome" taking hold with people who have sunk a lot of money into assets that are underperforming. I can't count the number of times I have heard someone—often someone otherwise very smart and astute—say something like, "Well, I bought XYZ stock at $60 and then it dropped to $40 and now it's sitting at $28. But I'm glad I bought it!" That is mind-boggling to me. They always have some sort of jargon to justify this feeling too, whether it's "cash flow" this or "book value" that. When it really comes down to it, however, they paid $60 for a $28 stock.

Much of this can be attributed to the "sunk-cost fallacy," a well-known human tendency to justify wasted money, sometimes by wasting more of it. It is also known as "throwing good money after bad." Few people want to admit that they made a mistake, and everyone wants to believe they can still turn a loser around (which, as we've established, investors have no power to do). All too often, though, these impulses cause us to dig a deeper hole rather than simply climbing out.

A similar fallacy, what we call the "anchor fallacy," plays on investors' greed. It goes like this: Someone buys a stock at $40 per share and it rockets up to $80 before falling back to $70. Many people will decide to wait until the stock goes back up to $80 before selling. And if the stock drifts down further, maybe to $50? Well, now the investor will wait until it climbs back up to $70. What if the stock plummets all the way to $20? The investor now has to wait until it gets back up to $40 because he needs to at least break even, after all. Although this can seem reasonable while it unfolds, it is clearly and objectively wrong-headed.

It's called the anchor fallacy because investors anchor their sell decisions to a historical high in price, and rather than deal with the reality of the declining price, they stay with it all the way down. As we've discussed before, historical precedent alone (the fact that a stock once traded much higher) is not a reliable predictor of future performance. Just because a stock once traded at $80 per share doesn't suggest it will ever reach such heights again.

This idea illustrates something really important about disasters: They are frequently slow to develop and often observable. A company going bankrupt is much more like a hurricane than an earthquake or a mudslide. There is no reason in the world you can't outrun a forecasted hurricane—unless, of course, you refuse to move.

When we think about stock disasters in recent memory, one springs immediately to mind: Enron. Almost as soon as Enron's stock price hit zero in December of 2001, narratives were already being spun about criminals and victims and how everyone was blindsided.

If you ask the typical investor, which I often do, how much time there was between Enron's peak at $80 per share and its fall to zero, most would say something like, "Weeks. Maybe a month or two." This is because we have been fed a narrative about an overnight upset that no one could have thought possible or seen coming. In reality, this is what Enron's price chart looked like over the course of that fateful year:

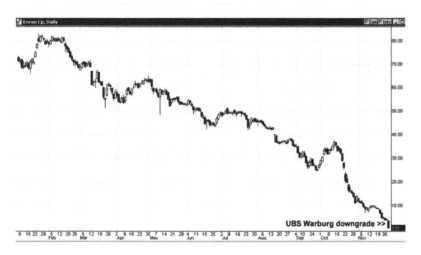

Source: TradeStation

As you can see, Enron investors had *at least* five months after the stock clearly started to decline (March–July) to get out at more than $50 per share, and as late as October investors could have gotten more than $30 per share. That fact is rarely mentioned when we talk about how Enron had everyone hoodwinked. In order for there to be helpless victims, the actual evidence must be ignored.

It is in Wall Street's best interest to develop these types of one-sided narratives because, if no one could possibly have known Enron could collapse, then Wall Street cannot be held responsible for failing to have acted. These folks want very much to say, "How could we have known?" And to do so they pretend there were no markers presaging the event. But in truth, if they had been following the stock price trend, it would have told them everything they needed to know: Something was very wrong at Enron.

Similarly, this reframing of the collapse absolves the investor—yes, the investor—of responsibility as well. It is absolutely true that financial advisors and their firms have a responsibility to protect and inform their clients, but who is ultimately responsible? If you give an advisor $10 million dollars and you wind up with $5 million, who is really to blame? If your money is at risk, you are ultimately responsible for its preservation.

Looking at the price chart, we see multiple places where a shareholder with any kind of sell discipline would have gotten out. If a trend follower had purchased Enron stock, for example, at $40 per share, he would have enjoyed that little boost in July. And when it began to fall again, that same investor would have sold it to preserve the profit. Even with falsified data coming from the upper echelon at Enron, the stock price trend offered the true story—it told investors that something was very wrong.

This is how the mantra of "Buy, Hold, and Hope" and the myth of quality stocks proving themselves hurts investors.

The simple truth of all this is that the only people who lost all their money in the Enron collapse were the people who refused to sell. The reason someone might refuse to sell a sinking stock is always emotional or subjective, because a fact-based analysis would always suggest that a stock that was acting the way Enron was acting in 2001 should be sold.

"Six Sigma" is a phrase originally used to describe a set of processes in manufacturing aimed at systematically eliminating the production of defective product. Wasting time, labor, or raw materials in manufacturing

The reason someone might refuse to sell a sinking stock is always emotional or subjective ...

flushes profits down the drain. One of the two most common methodologies is known as DMAIC.

The DMAIC project methodology has five phases:

Define the problem, and the project goals specifically.

Measure key aspects of the current process and collect relevant data.

Analyze the data to investigate and verify cause-and-effect relationships. Determine what the relationships are and attempt to ensure that all factors have been considered.

Improve or optimize the current process based upon data analysis or mistake-proofing.

Control the future process to ensure that any deviations from target are corrected before they result in defects. Implement control systems such as statistical process controls and continuously monitor the process.

Every manufacturing plant in the world aspires to Six Sigma recognition. Men and women in manufacturing who possess the coveted "Master Black Belt" designation are highly sought after and command premium salaries. The reason is simple: These folks understand and can implement the processes that eliminate waste, reduce risk, and maximize profits.

A robust trading system is a set of rules or procedures that accomplishes the same goals in portfolio management. The financial advisor's job is the same as the jobs of those Master Black Belts: eliminate waste, reduce risk, and maximize profits. While the comparison is imperfect, you can see how implementing a version of DMAIC in portfolio management would be very helpful.

We can use those same letters to spell out what an investment management system should do:

Define the goal (create profits; mitigate risks).

Measure and collect relevant data.

Analyze the data (portfolio construction).

Improve and optimize processes (ensure that variables remain relevant).

Control (implement systems that monitor portfolio management process, including disposition of stocks).

It is difficult to imagine the general manager of a successful manufacturing plant being unable to articulate mission-critical processes (what raw materials to buy, when to buy those materials, how much to buy, etc.). In portfolio management, it is mission-critical that the manager have processes that identify the following:

1. What securities to buy?
2. When to buy those securities?
3. How much of those securities to buy?
4. What to do with them as the future unfolds?

It is fair to say that the general manager of a manufacturing plant would never say, "We buy quality raw materials when we have the money, depending on how much is available." And yet, many money managers essentially give that answer to their clients, albeit with impressive words and phrases like "bottom up," "top down," "fundamentally undervalued," and "long-term." Unfortunately, impressive terminology adds no value to a portfolio.

That is why I am so adamant about not relying on subjective analysis. Don't lean on hunches or history, or on a connection to a company or a CEO, or on your love for a product. Focus on the actual tangible markers of impending failure and success. Your advisor should do everything in his power to remove his emotions—and the emotions of the client—from the equation and instead evaluate the situation as it really is. As a result, these critical investment decisions won't be colored by fear, hope, or a desire to save face.

CHAPTER SEVEN

Beyond the Market: Wealth Management

"I always wanted to be somebody, but now
I realize I should have been more specific."
—Lily Tomlin—

MONEY IS NEVER just about money. People, even very successful
people, wonder if they are doing the right things to take care
of themselves and their families. We worry about our children, and about how to prepare them for adulthood. Most
successful people I know wonder if they've done "enough."
This concern might focus on their retirement planning, but
just as often it's more than that. They want to know ... "Have
I done enough with my life?"

Money seeps into every part of a person's life, and it is
very difficult to successfully manage finances if they are com-
partmentalized from everything else.

I've seen every version of "rich." People who inherited money, people who made money, people who lost money and then made it back, people who handed their money off to a generation that wasn't prepared for it, and people who passed the torch to a generation that was capable of using it in positive and effective ways. If you're like most successful people, you don't want to leave this to chance. How do we stack the odds in favor of our families and our heirs? It starts with recognizing that it's probably not going to just take care of itself. Managing this process is what wealth management is all about.

What exactly is wealth management? CEG Worldwide, a consulting company to the financial services industry, defines it with this formula:

**Wealth Management = Investment Consulting
+ Advanced Planning + Relationship Management**

Their research indicates that portfolio management (investment consulting) is the number one concern of the affluent, as it should be. After portfolio management, they created this list, which goes in order of importance:

- Wealth Enhancement (mitigating taxes and improving cash flow)

- Wealth Transfer (making sure their assets go where they want them to go and that their heirs are provided for)
- Wealth Protection (ensuring that assets aren't unjustly taken)
- Charitable Giving (roughly one-third of the affluent are very interested and active in philanthropy)

Wealth management, then, encompasses all aspects of your financial affairs. Though it is easily the most important part, how your investments are managed is still just one aspect of overall wealth management.

These four secondary concerns are addressed in the advanced planning phase of wealth management. Each of these areas of concern requires the expertise of professionals from outside the investment consulting business. Generally, in order to achieve your family's financial goals you will need a trust and estate lawyer, a CPA, a life insurance specialist, and a property and casualty specialist. Each of these professionals has an important role to play in preparing and protecting your assets for maximum impact. To make sure your assets are properly titled for estate planning and asset protection purposes, you will need a trust and estate lawyer. To fund estate taxes you may need life insurance. To protect your assets from litigation risk, a property and casualty specialist is needed to assess those insurance needs. A CPA advises you on how to minimize your tax burden and improve cash flow. If philanthropy is important to you, your advisor, lawyer, and CPA will be helpful in structuring those gifts.

The final element of the wealth management process formula is relationship management. You might wonder what this has to do with accomplishing your financial goals. Well, unless you have a family office managing your financial affairs, the professionals whose services you will need to accomplish all that's important to you will not work together in the same office. They may not even know each other. Lawyers work at law firms, not at insurance agencies. That's why managing these professional relationships can be difficult and exhausting. It's no wonder that, according to CEG research, many affluent families haven't updated their estate plan in eight years. You would be surprised by the number of wealthy families that have done no planning at all. I think this is attributable to the overwhelming nature of managing the process.

That's where your financial advisor comes in. The financial advisor should be quite skilled at quarterbacking this process, and although he can't write a trust document for you, the advisor usually has a broad knowledge of what needs to be done to accomplish the four secondary concerns of the affluent. Further, most quality advisors actively cultivate relationships with the best professionals in the fields mentioned above. You may know whom you want to use, and you may only need someone to facilitate the process. If you don't know whom you want to use, however, and you need to start from scratch, your financial advisor should have the professionals in place to get the work done properly and at a reasonable price.

Having a financial advisor at the center of this process will likely make it run more smoothly, and possibly more cost-effectively, than if you do it yourself. Why is this the case? Because the best professional service providers get the lion's share of their new business through referrals from other professionals, it is very important that they deliver a great client experience every time. While I can't speak for all professional service providers, I can tell you that many of us view referring professionals as very important clients. An accountant who refers a half dozen clients a year to an estate planning attorney is very important to that attorney. When I think about the experiences I've had with doctors to whom I've been referred by other doctors, I realize that I'm always treated more quickly than I would have been if I had walked in off the street. The same principle is in play here.

We've established that the market is indifferent to your goals, hopes, and dreams. But that doesn't mean your advisor should ignore the plans you have for your life, your family, and your money. As we've discussed, the financial services industry has a tendency to over-generalize concepts. Buy-and-hold proponents overlook the reality that the market can produce negative returns for significant periods of time, and proponents of tactical investing tend to minimize the importance of goal setting and financial planning. The investor is best served when robust planning and goal setting are accomplished in conjunction with tactical investment systems designed to capture the upside of positive global trends while diminishing the wealth-crushing impact of negative trends.

Have you ever been to a restaurant that was simply perfect? The menu is unique and the portions are just right, as is the presentation. The staff is knowledgeable and courteous. They are helpful but not overbearing. There's no pressure to order the "starter" and no hard sales pitch for dessert. This doesn't happen by accident; everything is perfectly choreographed, and yet it comes off as natural and effortless. Nothing is rushed, and yet there's no wasted time or wasted words. If you'd like to linger and enjoy dessert and coffee, that's perfect. If you'd rather get in and get out, that's great too. The ambiance, service, selection, and quality are constant, but the customer determines how he or she will experience the evening.

This is exactly the sort of experience you should expect from a great wealth and investment management company. The goal of every financial advisor should be to deliver a great experience by creating an environment that enables the client to enjoy the benefits of what the company offers in the way that best suits him or her as an individual.

Now, imagine that you've eaten at a great restaurant 100 times and have enjoyed it each time. Then on the 101st time you eat there, you get food poisoning and spend the next few nights in the hospital. In deference to your long-standing relationship with the restaurant's owners, perhaps you give them another shot. Then, after 50 more great meals in a row—*bam!* Back to the hospital. Unless your son owns the place, you won't be eating there again. That's essentially what's happened to buy-and-hold investors over the last fourteen years. Twice they have had several years of great returns (food) followed by a huge decline that wiped out the gains (food poisoning). As of today, the buy-and-hold "restaurant" has had another almost six-year run with pretty good food.

Thankfully, just as there are Michelin-starred restaurants with welcoming staffs and consistently great food, you can find an advisor who offers astute financial guidance coupled with a genuine desire to take care of the investor's total financial experience.

My next statement frequently induces eye rolls, but it really is true: Money brings with it a whole host of problems—problems that those without it will never have. These are perhaps "better" problems to have, but they still represent hurdles that the most successful families must address proactively.

The very wealthy often build their lives around the advantages that money creates. Wealthy people can have multiple homes; some travel extensively, and many fly privately. They are the minority and they know it. So why would they ever content themselves with the same financial strategies the majority is using?

A family in this country with an income of $200,000 per year should be perfectly comfortable. But the idea of buying a Mercedes-Benz for the new high school graduate is out of the question. It's an automatic "no," and not because they don't want him to have the car; they simply can't afford it. But when a family *can* afford to make those purchases—when they can afford almost anything—how do they learn to say no? *When* do they say no? And why? If their personal economy does not impose limits, the investors have to define their own limits—and then enforce them.

People who aren't wealthy do not have to worry that their children will be negatively affected by their proximity to abstract money—i.e., money that they didn't participate in earning. They do not worry about raising kids with a sense of entitlement who feel they have "earned" what is really just an accident of birth. Raising children who are not dependent on their wealthy parents—or puffed up with monstrous egos—and who can grow into successful contributors to society in their own right is no small feat. We all know the rich kid who was "born on third base and thought he hit a triple."

I have seen parents who shower their children with everything they could possibly want, giving them access to huge wealth before they're mature enough to fully understand and manage it. And I have seen good kids turn into self-important sponges with no goals or direction of their own. These children, once full of promise, can struggle for a lifetime.

By the same token, I have also seen parents who erred too far in the other direction and unnecessarily deprived their children of access to capital. If you don't invest in your child's promising future, then what is the point of having money? It is possible to be so afraid of raising entitled children that you can effectively rob them of the legitimate benefits of your economic success.

This is an incredibly delicate balance to strike, and it's something almost all of my clients with children have expressed concern about. How do you invest in your children without simply handing them a pile of money? How do you use your resources constructively? How can your money be

How do you invest in your children without simply handing them a pile of money? How do you use your resources constructively? How can your money be a positive influence on the lives of those you love?

a positive influence on the lives of those you love? How do you avoid lording your money over your kids, or worse yet, buying their affection? I've seen many a divorce in which the former spouses use their bank accounts to win a child's favor. In the end, it's a toxic situation for everyone.

These are difficult and frightening questions because there are no do-overs when it comes to parenting. If you lose money in the stock market—even a lot of money—perhaps you can make a comeback. If unbridled access to wealth ruins your child, or if they miss out on some critical experience that might have turned them into a good, hardworking adult—that is much more difficult to fix. You can never recoup those losses.

These are some of the issues you may encounter as you go through the advanced planning phase of wealth management. (By the way, this isn't a "one and done" deal; ongoing planning is necessary for most affluent families.) You and your spouse, in conjunction with your trusted advisors, can proactively plan how you are going to handle certain situations as they present themselves. These advisors can tell you how other families have successfully handled similar situations. You can't plan for every possible contingency, but you can develop guidelines that will help you navigate life as the future unfolds. You can meet family challenges head on, and rather than just hoping it all works out, you can affect the direction of the lives of those most important to you.

Just as watching a stock price can reveal that a company might be in trouble, there are certain markers in relationships that you should not ignore. The earlier a problem is detected, the quicker a solution can be found and implemented, increasing the probability of a favorable outcome for everyone involved.

CHAPTER EIGHT

Stress-Testing Your Portfolio

"Everybody has a plan until
I hit them in the mouth."
—Mike Tyson—

WHEN A NEW client comes to meet with us, we suggest an exercise that illustrates the potential benefit of tactical investing and the potential danger of buy-and-hold as the sole investment discipline. We call it the Portfolio Stress Test, and it's not unlike a stress test you might undergo with your cardiologist ... only it's not you on the treadmill.

In our test we analyze all of the assets (stocks, bonds, mutual funds, and alternative investments) as they exist now and then impose a set of conditions that provide "stress." In this case, test the assets against the big downturn of 2008, and determine how the investments would fare in a similar circumstance.

The test looks much like this:

Fund Category	2008 Return	Beginning Value	Ending Value
Muni California Interm	-4.45%	$430,000.00	$410,865.00
Diversified Emerging Markets	-54.50%	$81,733.33	$37,188.67
Diversified Emerging Markets	-49.20%	$81,733.33	$41,520.53
Diversified Emerging Markets	-53.57%	$81,733.33	$37,948.79
Foreign Small/Mid Blend	-43.92%	$191,866.67	$107,598.83
Real Estate	-37.36%	$307,200.00	$192,430.08
Small Blend	-38.43%	$316,000.00	$191,852.12
Foreign Small/Mid Value	-41.42%	$191,866.67	$112,395.49
Large Blend	-35.53%	$634,200.00	$408,868.74
Foreign Large Value	-44.38%	$191,866.67	$106,716.24
Large Value	-41.57%	$634,200.00	$370,563.06
Small Value	-37.76%	$311,600.00	$193,939.84
Muni California Interm	-5.96	$430,000.00	$404,372.00
Cash	0.00%	$120,000.00	$120,000.00
2008 ROR	**-31.59%**	**$3,999.600.00**	**$2,736,259.39**

Source: TradeStation

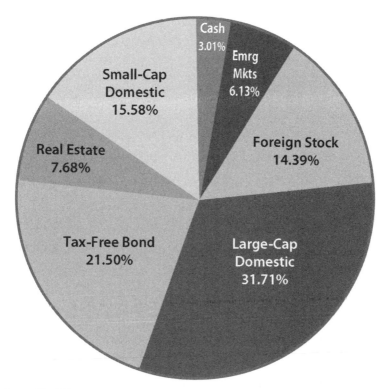

Source: TradeStation

Though most investors actually remember experiencing the downturn of 2008 firsthand, it's quite startling to see the impact a cyclical bear market can have on the typical investment portfolio. It's important that people have a real and practical understanding of what it would mean for them to lose big in the market. Investors should also see the sort of growth they could expect given future rates of return on their current asset mix. What's interesting is how much more a bear market negatively affects the portfolio than a bull market positively affects it.

The question then becomes, "What are you going to do about it?"

We can't say when the next big downturn will happen, and we can't say how bad it's going to be. People are quick to dismiss the example of the Great Depression, certain that kind of decline could never, ever happen again. But I think it's delusional to argue that an event that has already happened once could never happen again.

The Great Depression represents the greatest single decline the market has ever seen: about 88 percent from 1929 to 1932.

Much of the public considers the last cyclical bear market (2008–2009) to be something that could never happen again. Given the magnitude of the declines experienced in the Depression, in the dot-com bubble, and in the most recent financial crisis, are we wise to think the market might never have a similar decline? Okay, maybe it won't. But "maybe" is a far cry from "absolutely." It is certainly a possibility, and one we simply cannot afford to ignore. If we do ignore it, we do so at our peril.

Even if nothing that drastic happens, are you willing to simply stand back and take whatever the market dishes out? Are you content to sit idly by while your investments are obliterated? And what would losing that amount of money really mean to you?

When an investor does our exercise, it's more than just a stress test for his portfolio; it becomes a test of his future. How would your relationships be affected if you suddenly lost 60 percent of your wealth? Would you still be able to retire happily and comfortably with your spouse? Would you be forced to cancel your plans to purchase that beautiful family vacation home you've been wanting for years? These are real questions that have to be asked, even if contemplating such a situation is uncomfortable. Any time a massive upset occurs, those who are affected by it look to assign blame. Maybe they blame the market, Wall Street, or other external factors, but many of them take their frustration out on the family member who oversees their investments.

Financial difficulties have a way of putting stress on all the weak points of a marriage and family—at the bare minimum, they aren't improving anything. Plus, when people become accustomed to living with a certain degree of affluence, it can be very difficult to adjust to a new standard of living. It can prove impossible in some cases. Trust me. I've seen it.

Many people know about these risks in the abstract, though they can rarely imagine these kinds of things actually happening to them. They accept the risks because they have been told again and again that they have to. After all, if you want to make money in the market, according to buy-and-hold advisors, you have to accept all the risk of the market. I frequently ask investors to imagine they have $10 million. Imagine you have had the money long enough to have built a lifestyle around the assets. Now, what would affect your life more: suddenly having $20 million, or suddenly having $5 million?

Wall Street has mastered selling the fear of missing out. You will often hear that if you miss the ten best days in the stock market, you could lose 80 percent of your returns. Let's look at that warning another way: What would your returns be if you missed the ten worst days? No one ever raises that question. My point is not that you should expect to miss the worst ten days for the market—or that it's even possible to do so—but that Wall Street selectively uses data that supports the buy-and-hold philosophy upon which their business model is dependent. Wall Street needs investors to stay essentially fully invested at all times, and statistics like this, while perhaps true in fact, are misleading and miss the point. It presents the classic false choice: Invest in the market long-term (translation: never reduce exposure to stocks) or be a greedy and foolish day trader. In reality, there are far more options than this extreme dichotomy suggests.

As we've discussed, many investors have as their investment objective some version of "Beat the market." You might be asking yourself, "What else could it be?" Let me give you a few objectives that may work for you:

1. Compound your capital in a meaningful way over time.
2. Minimize the scope and duration of downturns in your account.
3. Recover lost capital quickly once the downturn ends.

I'll make a few observations about these three objectives. First, there is no mention of the stock market, its return, or "beating" it in any way. Second, if you accomplish these objectives, you will have far more money than you started with because you will have spent less time losing money in bear markets and more time making new capital.

How do you accomplish this? Your process needs to address the critical elements of portfolio management. Here are its four primary components:

1. What securities to buy?
2. When to buy those securities?
3. How much of those securities to buy?
4. What to do with them as the future unfolds?

I'll give you a system that answers those questions right now. It's *very* simple. You must remember, though, that there are no perfect systems. No one system will work in every type of market. That's why it's important to diversify the systems used to manage your investments (as opposed to simply diversifying the assets you hold). So here are the answers:

1. What to buy?
   • SPY (S&P 500)
2. When to buy it?
   • When it is trading over the 200-day moving average.
3. How much to buy?
   • 25 percent of the value of your account.
4. When to sell it?
   • When it trades below the 200-day moving average.

By using this simple system, the investor will be invested in the market during a big cyclical bull market and out during a cyclical bear market. Remember, we never know how far the market will go in either direction. A system like this takes the pressure off deciding when to buy and when to sell. Can you lose money using this system? Yes. Is it possible to get "whip sawed" from time to time? Yes. Should you abandon all other investment disciplines for this method? Of course not. This system will work well in the kind of market we've been in for the last fourteen years, a market characterized by trends in both directions that have lasted for several years. It won't work very well in a "choppy" market like the one we had during the 1970s.

When we look at these stress tests, the cost of not changing anything becomes clear. These are the kinds of losses investors can see when they stick with the buy-and-hold model. I am always wary (as I think most people are) of those who present themselves as infallible or their products and systems as a magic bullet. While I believe the "costs" of tactical investment systems are well worth it, there are certain market environments that are less favorable to these strategies. In fact, the last several years have been difficult for some tactical managers and pure trend followers when compared to buy-and-hold.

The problem with being proactive about protecting capital is that sometimes measures are taken to avoid a potential danger that never fully materializes. Remember, your objectives don't have to include outperforming the market—which, as I've shown, you could accomplish while still losing a lot of money.

There are times when (looking back) having 100 percent exposure to the market would have been the best position to take. It's tempting to think this way, and it takes discipline to resist the temptation to second-guess the systems and strategies designed to protect and grow wealth. It's like saying, "If I'd bought ABC before it was bought out by XYZ, I would've

... there's not a sailor worth his salt who would simply stay the course in the face of gale-force winds—he knows the course must be managed according to current conditions.

made millions." It's true, but what does it matter? This kind of Monday-morning quarterbacking is only possible with the benefit of hindsight. If we see objective indications that a stock is in trouble and liquidate the position, only to watch it rally, some would say we made a mistake. But was it really a mistake? I think that's a bit like saying it was a mistake to wear a life vest on your successful Colorado River canoeing trip. True, nothing bad happened and the vest probably made it harder to paddle, but the potential consequence of not wearing the vest (drowning) makes the inconvenience of wearing it a small price to pay.

If you look back at the period from January 2000 through February 2013, that point becomes clear. If you had been in the S&P 500 for this thirteen-year period, you would barely have broken even. The investment industry likes to tell you that if you just stay in the market for the long term, you'll earn an average annual return of 10 to 11 percent. But the fallacy of the 10 to 11 percent average return is that it uses an eighty-year average. This may work for you if you have the lifespan of a giant tortoise, but most people have no more than a twenty-year horizon. Who cares about eighty years? Those twenty years are the only ones that matter.

Looking back, there are long periods during which the market provided little or no return:

1929—the market took twenty-five years to break even
1966—the market took sixteen years to break even
1973—the market took ten years to break even
2000—the market took thirteen years to break even
(it briefly regained the 2000 highs in November of 2007 before plummeting 56 percent over the next sixteen months)

Although looking back can't tell us what will happen in the future, it can certainly tell us what *could* happen. That being said, there's not a sailor worth his salt who would simply stay the course in the face of gale-force winds—he knows the course must be managed according to current conditions.

The same can be said about investing. When conditions allow, we position portfolios for growth. And when market conditions require it, we work to preserve capital.

We are all driven by the emotions of fear and greed. In a nice bull market, greed is the overwhelming emotion, and after a bear market begins, fear becomes the dominant emotion. From September of 2008 until March of 2009, abject fear was the predominant emotion. It should come as no surprise that equity mutual fund redemptions were at some of the highest levels ever in March of that year. Legitimate fear isn't a bad thing. Fear is an instinctive, God-given survival skill. The problem is that, at least in behavioral finance, human beings have a hard time discerning situations that are dangerous to them from those that are less so. The time to plan for crisis is not in the midst of crisis.

At bottom, the "Buy, Hold, and Hope" strategies have no plan for crisis. The strategy is predicated on it all working out in the end. It's interesting that people generally feel the best about investing after markets go up a lot. As of this writing (literally as I type), the S&P 500 is putting in a new high. It seems to me that stock market risk is greater today than it was in March of 2009 at its bottom, and yet investors are more confident today than at any time since 2007. It's virtually indisputable that the primary beneficiary of the economic stimulus in this country and abroad has been the global financial markets. The markets will account for that at some point, perhaps when quantitative easing (the policy of the Federal Reserve to buy US treasury bonds with newly printed money) is over. Today, stock market volatility is as low as it's been since late 2007. Low volatility indicates a lack of fear, which in the past has presaged market tops. This is typical of human behavior after outsized gains in the market. We feel better after a period of good times and worse after a period of bad times. We would do well to exercise discretion when we are optimistic, not when we are pessimistic.

The world's best golfers will tell you their success when the Green Jacket is on the line is determined by staying true to their predetermined routine for each shot. The pre-swing routine is critical to proper execution. It doesn't always produce the desired results, but it certainly improves the probability of a desired outcome. You also have to know which club to use for each shot—you wouldn't use a driver in a green side bunker.

Everyone must decide what their priorities are and what their comfort level is. These decisions are personal. I believe, however, that tactical investment systems appeal more to common sense than does "Buy, Hold, and Hope."

Of course, we all have much more to invest than just money. In the last few years, it has become increasingly clear that my daughter is an incredibly talented singer/songwriter. Although she is still young, she is very good.

We always supported her, and as she grew older and more serious about her talents, we began to sense that a larger "stage" could give her all the opportunities she would need to become successful.

That's why, when some music industry professionals found out about her and asked to have a meeting in Los Angeles, we were willing to go. We took the whole family out to LA for the winter, rented an apartment, and had a series of meetings with music executives. While we were there, I also evaluated Greater LA as a potential location for an office of our firm.

By the end of our visit, it was clear our family loved California, and I felt comfortable operating there professionally. We also believed that both Grace and our son Clayton would thrive in this new environment. Joy and I had come to a juncture where we had to decide how we were going to invest our time, energy, and resources. Before we made our decision, we took a good look at the relevant indicators of success.

The entertainment world is not exactly like the market, and chance plays a huge role in whether or not an individual becomes successful. However, I could at least try to get an objective analysis of my daughter's talents. Every father thinks his child is wonderful, and I didn't want us to overestimate our daughter's potential.

When I was a kid, my parents would have been insane to pack up and move to help me pursue a music or sports career. That certainly hasn't stopped some parents, but we didn't want to make that mistake. So we asked outsiders and industry professionals if our daughter has what it takes. They all agreed that she was uniquely talented and could be very successful, given the right timing and opportunities.

These days, she is maturing as an artist, writing and recording regularly. She has worked with Grammy-winning songwriters—something made possible by our move to California. Once again, we can't see into the future, and there's no telling whether she will become a professional musician or head off in an altogether different direction. She is still young, and there are so many ways this could go.

However, when we had to make the decision, we objectively evaluated all the available data, including her skill level, her passion for music, the value of relocating to LA, and the cost of the move. What we've received has been remarkable. Our son Clayton is an honor roll student, a regular actor in the community theatre, and a budding musician in his own right. We live five blocks from the kids' school and less than two miles from my office. Our kids' friends come from all over the world. Our dinner table is a veritable United Nations, with kids from Brazil, Germany, Japan, and England routinely gathered around it. And we've actually simplified our lives by moving from Mississippi to California. Who would ever have guessed that could happen?

Taking risks is a necessary and rewarding part of life, and sometimes the riskier

Taking risks is a necessary and rewarding part of life, and sometimes the riskier ventures provide the greatest returns.

ventures provide the greatest returns. I believe we can temper that risk with intelligent analysis and a consistent set of rules, giving us the highest probability of success. If your investment strategy doesn't have a mechanism for protecting you in a big down market, maybe it's time to re-evaluate before it's too late.

CHAPTER NINE

What Do You Really Want?

"The two most important days in your life are the day you are born and the day you find out why."
—Mark Twain—

THE MOST IMPORTANT thing we do in our initial consultation with clients is to discover what's important to them. We need to know what it is about money that the client values so we can position them to get the most utility from their investments. That's really the only reason to have wealth, isn't it? Your money should help you accomplish that which is most important to you.

Everyone has unique goals that can only be attained with the help of customized plans. Is your objective to enjoy the fruits of your labor as much as possible during your lifetime? Is your objective to "die broke," enjoying or giving away all your assets in the course of your lifetime?

Everyone wants to leave a legacy, but not everyone wants to leave the same legacy. Establishing a family foundation to fund education initiatives is a different undertaking than creating a family office where your children and grandchildren can invest and collectively run their money.

Some of us want to insulate ourselves and our families from downside potential as much as possible. Others are looking to make as much money as possible. Everyone has expectations, plans, and needs from their assets, but many investors don't even consciously know what those expectations are.

It's a blind spot, but it's certainly not irreversible. A lot of investors have simply never asked themselves the right questions. When pressed, they find it hard to articulate how their current wealth management strategy is furthering their goals—or even, concretely, what those goals are.

To develop the right strategy for accomplishing all that's important to you, it's necessary to ask yourself some important questions. In Chapter 8 we discussed the essential elements of portfolio management:

1. What securities to buy?
2. When to buy those securities?
3. How much of those securities to buy?
4. What to do with them as the future unfolds?

You remember these mission-critical elements, right? Well, questions like the ones below are of equal importance if you are serious about getting what you want out of your financial life. A financial advisor should be able to guide you through this process.

These questions may seem vague, but I promise that you will not accomplish your goals if you don't know what motivates you.

1. Values
What's important to you about money?

2. Goals
What would you like to see as your top accomplishments? What do you want to do for your children? What do you want to do for the world at large?

3. Relationships
Which family relationships mean the most to you? How important are your business and community relationships?

4. Assets
What is your source of income? Is it likely to change in the next few years? What are your

investment holdings? Explain your strategy for handling investments the way you do. When you think of your finances, what are your three biggest worries?

5. Advisors

Do you have a lawyer? How do you feel about that relationship? Do you have an insurance agent? A CPA or general accountant? An Investment Advisor?

6. Process

How involved do you want to be in your finances? How often would you like to meet to discuss your investments?

7. Interests

What do you like to do when you're not working or managing your financial affairs?

As I get to know my clients, I like to find out which of their accomplishments have given them the most satisfaction and what their strongest beliefs are. Is this someone who is going to want to leave a huge endowment to her alma mater?

Or someone who wants to donate a legacy to his church? It's my job to find out.

One client, when asked what he wanted to do for the world at large, said, "I want to make them laugh." That's a real thing to want to accomplish, especially for a guy who can do it. But he also had goals that were closer to home. "I want my children to know their dad loves them," he told me. "I want to help my boys become good men."

Another client wants to have a tennis court and get her black belt in karate. She also wants to use her life experience and financial resources to help children around the world deal effectively with the stresses caused by poverty and political unrest in their countries. This remarkable woman wants to give these kids practical coping skills that they can use every day to improve the quality of their lives, even in the midst of difficult external circumstances.

I have a client who is determined to eradicate illiteracy and has earmarked $100 million to accomplish that goal. Another client was moved to give millions of dollars to an organization that meets the needs of the fatherless in our nation's inner cities. But he doesn't just give money; he also volunteers his time every week with boys who have no positive male role model in their lives. These kids have no idea how much money the man gives (or if he gives any at all), but they know how much time he continues to invest in their lives. Is it possible to calculate the return on an investment like that? I don't think so.

These goals have nothing to do with asset allocation or bull and bear markets. They have everything to do with the imprint your life leaves on the people most important to you and on the world around you.

Some things simply will not get done unless you do them. The creator of the universe has tasked you with making a unique difference, whether it's for a certain grand cause or for one certain little girl. What joy it brings to those who figure out their life's purpose and act on it!

It's also important for you to be clear about what you like to do. Chances are you are not constrained by the economic pressures that affect most Americans. If you are a racecar enthusiast, it may be entirely feasible for you to purchase a number of Formula 1 racecars. If you love golf, you could reasonably travel the world, playing a round on every golf course that has ever hosted a major tournament. You can design your own woodland cabin or beachfront bungalow. The only way to make these big enterprises a reality is to clearly define the goal and get it down on paper. The affluent can afford to do the things they want to do; it is simply a matter of ensuring that their money will get them there efficiently and with minimal risk. If your advisor knows what sort of endpoint you are working toward, she can manage the money in a specific, tactical way that gives you the best probability of a positive outcome.

A good way to approach this is to work backwards, from the end to the beginning. Where you want to end up tomorrow necessarily determines the direction you start moving in today. Paint the picture of your life five, ten, or twenty years from today. If you were to write the end of your story, how would it read? Investors need to articulate their ideal outcomes, and everyone's ideal outcome is different.

I've had clients tell me they want to send their exceptionally bright child to an Ivy League school. I've had other clients tell me about a child who is great with his hands but not particularly academically inclined. That person's ideal does not include Harvard or Yale; it may not include college at all. Perhaps the child wants to go into a trade right away.

By permission Steve Breen and Creators Syndicate, Inc

Funding an education that ends with a PhD is not inherently better than making sure your son or daughter has technical experience in a trade. In fact, you should not be disappointed or feel uneasy if your child wants to go to trade school. Both college and trade schools are respectable ways to receive an education, and there are many ways for your son or daughter to make money with either opportunity. However, each of those different educational goals requires its own unique plan of action.

It may well cost a half-million dollars to educate a kid from high school through a PhD. While it's true that vocational training to be a master electrician costs far less than Harvard tuition, the expenses one might accrue on that path are less obvious than the academic route. What is this kid going to do with his vocational training? Perhaps he has business acumen in addition to being a skilled tradesman. Maybe he would like to open his own business. He may very well need $200,000 in start-up capital or a co-sign on a loan.

At the end of the day, preparing these two very different children to enter the workforce might work out to roughly the same expenditure. These are the sorts of calculations you should begin making, years or even decades before those numbers are ever called to account.

Differing individual goals are all equally valid, whether it be sailing around the world or building homes for Habitat for Humanity. The value comes from what those activities would mean to the individual *as a person*. If someone has dreamed his whole life of going into space and he begins planning to do just that, his goal is just as important as someone else's goal to make clean water more available in sub-Saharan Africa. If that's what motivates you to get up in the morning, great!

Everyone has a different set of priorities and a different approach to money. Many people never discover what it is they truly want to do because they are so caught up in what they *have* to do.

Most of us are busy, day in and day out. We have families to raise, businesses to build, lives to lead. This process may be your first opportunity to actually investigate hopes and dreams that have been left on the backburner for most of your life.

It's a very big world out there, but wealth has a way of shrinking it so that it can be fully experienced and enjoyed. This doesn't mean people with fewer resources can't dream big, because they absolutely can. You might be surprised just how many people could technically "afford" to spend six months backpacking through Europe. A trip like that is not as prohibitively expensive as one might imagine. However, if you have less wealth, these big enterprises come at the expense of other things.

You need to nail down the nature and the cost of what it is you want to do. Even for the very wealthy, these things do have a cost. They have a financial cost, a personal cost, and most important, they cost us time. If people are fully informed about what their would-be dream requires of them, they can make educated choices about how to allocate their resources.

Over the years I've observed an interesting phenomenon that often takes place when people don't ask themselves the important questions about what they want. Because they do not think deeply about these things in their daily lives, they often develop conflicting objectives. For example, let us return to our spaceman. If he really wants to undertake his plan, he is looking at a financial cost of tens of millions of dollars. Now, if he is worth a billion dollars he can afford it, if getting into space is his priority. But spending that money will affect other decisions in his life.

Spaceman won't have to sell a house or buy a cheaper car, but he will have to think long and hard before doing that $250 million real estate development deal later in the year. This process crystallizes everything the client is "shooting for" and reveals the places where a person's objectives might come into conflict.

The goal of wealth management is to allocate our finite resources in a way that accomplishes our heart's desire. If we don't use our money to go after what we most long for, then why on earth do we have it? Your heart's desire probably won't look like anyone else's, because it is unique to you. Maybe you have a deep and abiding need to give to and invest in other people. Maybe your dream is about exploring new frontiers.

Sometimes, in the course of this process, people will realize they don't really want to do what they thought they wanted to do. Often this happens when people have only a vague sense of their goals, and a poor understanding of what accomplishing those goals would actually entail.

Your goal here is to be honest and intentional. Instead of having a generalized, unarticulated goal, you want to have a clear, precise, and objective goal and plan of action. The way to really affect the outcome is to make cogent, intentional choices.

If your money is doing what it's supposed to do, it will pave the way from point A to B, from the life you have now to the life you dream of having. It's not in your best interest to let your money sit idly while you cross your fingers and hope for the best. Instead, take careful and measured action and design the road map to accomplish all that's important to you.

CHAPTER TEN

Wrap It Up

"I think I can, I think I can ..."
—The Little Engine that Could—

IT'S OFTEN SAID that the greatest luxury money can buy is not having to think about money. In my line of work, I've found this to be true. Overwhelmingly, my clients are people who don't want to think about their money. They do not want to spend time and mental energy making sure they are in good financial shape. They want someone to tell them everything is okay, and—this is critical—they want everything to actually *be* okay.

Successful people want time to experience things and to create things. Although traditional retirement is usually not a concern for the affluent, they often experience a change in lifestyle as they age. Perhaps they want to travel more, or spend more time with their children or their spouse. Some want to become more active in their communities or explore new hobbies and passions. Virtually all of them want to build something that is greater than themselves—their goal is to create a significant legacy. These are people with a deep desire to give back.

They cannot do this if they are worried about losing large chunks of their wealth. To be able to throw themselves whole-heartedly into these new ventures, not only do they need to feel secure, they need to have the time and energy to devote to other pursuits. These are not the sorts of people who want to putter around, micromanaging every detail of their investment portfolio. They want to live the meaningful, exciting lives their wealth has enabled them to live. They want to be able to trust the people they hire to manage their assets so they can legitimately delegate those tasks. Like most things, wealth is a relative notion. How someone else defines wealth isn't all that important to you. What's important is that *your* wealth, however much that may be, is wisely managed.

Essentially, all wealth and investment managers have the very same set of tools: stocks, bonds, cash, real assets like real estate, precious metals, etc. That's the standard set of products we have to work with. What sets a good financial strategy apart is **how** and **when** those tools are deployed and in what proportion. It's a little bit like chemistry: You can combine the same basic ingredients, but whether you wind up with salt or mustard gas depends on the ratios and the external conditions.

I find that many investors are increasingly concerned about the buy-and-hold investment strategy. Many of them are uncomfortable with the way the internal logic of buy-and-hold flies in the face of everything they know about good decision-making. They are worried about being asked to put their money into the stock market, wondering whether the market will give them the returns they need when it matters most. It's worth repeating that the market is indifferent to your goals and schedule. You must deal with the market on its terms—not the other way around.

Our clients are people who are tired of relying on luck when their most significant dreams are on the line. They want the reassurance of a clear plan that prepares for potential disasters. They are looking for a more thoughtful approach to maximizing opportunity and managing risk.

Not only do retired people want this more analytical approach—they absolutely require it. Many wealthy people devote less

... the market is indifferent to your goals and schedule.

time to earning money when they feel they have created enough wealth and are "done." Unfortunately, if their money is exposed to the market during a cyclical bear market, they could very well find themselves *un-done* in just a few short years. We all saw people retire in the decade before the 2008 downturn, good and hard-working folks who thought they were financially prepared for the rest of their lives, only to find half their net worth destroyed just a few short years later.

It's not just the market that can derail your future plans. Many a fortune has been lost to bad investments in private companies, or just simple lifestyle bloat. If you aren't actively earning new income, you should be cognizant of how you are spending the money you have. How many times have we heard that old story of someone getting rich and then, just a few short years later, going broke and suffocating under massive debt? How many actors, musicians, or athletes have gone from having tens of millions of dollars to being flat broke in a seemingly impossible span of time? How is it that some people become suddenly wealthy and just as suddenly poor? For one thing, they didn't know how to deal with the overwhelming number of people who suddenly wanted a piece of the pie. Take Vince Young, for example: In 2006 he was a first-round draft choice out of the University of Texas who earned more than $30 million playing mostly for the Tennessee Titans. In 2013 he filed for bankruptcy. Why? He didn't know how to be rich.

Most of us don't live the rags-to-riches storyline of the professional athlete. More likely, you're the businessman or woman who built a successful company over thirty years and recently sold it. You want to enjoy life in a different way. Now there's a small (or large) fortune that must be managed. You also have a ton of time on your hands. The income that supported your lifestyle is gone, and so is the work that occupied your time for your entire adult life. It's not an easy transition from CEO to retiree—those who've done it will testify to that.

It is shockingly easy to lose money, always far easier than it is to make it.

It is shockingly easy to lose money, always far easier than it is to make it. If you want to protect your money—especially if you aren't actively making more—you have to have a plan in place. It is not enough to simply trust the vicissitudes of the market. You need to have a system for reaping the benefits of good markets while still protecting yourself from the ravages of bad markets.

You also need someone who understands the unique circumstances of significant wealth and the special challenges the very wealthy face. The right financial advisor can also serve as a buffer between her clients and people who are looking for funding for a new business. If a cousin has a great idea to open a restaurant, or a niece needs capital for a start-up, the client can defer to the wealth management firm as the "heavy." Emotionally, it's easier to tell a loved one "no" if you can put some of the blame on another party. Often "My financial advisor doesn't think it's a good idea" is more palatable than "I don't want to." In this way, investors can protect themselves without sowing discord among family and friends.

Nine times out of ten, these "opportunities" are not good ideas. Most of these ventures fail, simply because the majority of new ventures fail.

As a rule, people tend to overestimate the value they bring to an enterprise and forget the help and good fortune they had along the way. They look back at their success, and over time it becomes a story of how their inherent talents triumphed, rather than a struggle that involved a lot of hard work, some good fortune, and the efforts of many, many people. Having experienced so much personal success, these people see nothing to contradict their resolute feeling that they are uniquely intelligent and talented (which they may well be) and that their talents are widely applicable (which they usually aren't).

Wherever there is wealth, there will be people standing in line to become yes-men. There is money to be made in agreeing with every idea conceived by the very wealthy. The best financial advisors can help you ferret out the truly great ideas from the ones that are likely to rob you of your time, or worse.

As we discussed in Chapter 6, we all have biases at work when we make any decision, big or small. Like everyone, I've fallen prey to my own biases and have paid a big price for doing so. Before moving to California, we put our house in Mississippi on the market. We priced it at what we thought was a fair price, but in hindsight I see that we had "anchored" the asking price to a favorable appraisal we'd gotten some years before. We ignored what the market was telling us about the value of our house and stubbornly refused to lower the price.

By the time we did lower the price, the house had been on the market for such a long time that we couldn't generate any excitement about it. Because of our emotional attachment to the house, we couldn't see that it simply wasn't worth what we thought it was worth. After years of making mortgage payments on a house we didn't live in, we finally

Wherever there is wealth, there will be people standing in line to become yes-men.

sold it for 30 percent less than we could have if had we had priced it right to begin with.

I share that story as a way of letting you know that I am not immune to personal bias. I know very well how scary it is when an asset drops in value far more than you ever imagined possible. But when these biases are at work, things become hazy and unclear. Not only is it a losing proposition at present; there's the unpleasant reality that it could get much worse later. In the oil and gas exploration business, they say, "There are much worse things than a dry hole." That means it's far better to know something's not working than to be unaware that it's not working.

I see a lot of people who assume they are doing everything right because they happened to catch the right market at the right time. Only when the bottom falls out do they realize how bad things can get.

It is in those moments that they turn to their financial advisor for advice. What happens when that advisor can only tell them to "hang on" and keep doing the same things they've been doing all along? What happens when it becomes clear that the "expert" has no better sense of what should be done than you?

Shouldn't you ask these questions now so you won't have to in the midst of a crisis? It is far better to work through the worst-case scenario in theory than to encounter it in practice.

Does it seem wise to leave your financial future to chance? The right wealth management process can help you design the rest of your life for maximum impact, however you define that. Goal setting and planning are vitally important to achieving all that's important to you. Of course, you know what they say about the "best-laid plans of mice and men," and it's true: planning will only take you so far. As we've established, the markets do not care one whit about you personally, or about your goals. In the face of this, you must be proactive if you want to be preemptive.

A bear market cycle can cause those best-laid plans to unravel—and there's no way to prevent a bear market from happening. There *is*, however, a way to plan for it and to protect your assets accordingly. Tactical portfolio management in conjunction with robust goal setting and planning is a rational approach to charting your financial future. It's a powerful combination.

If you've enjoyed this book, I invite you to reach out to me and continue the conversation. You can visit my web site at www.rogercdavis.com, or e-mail me directly at roger.davis@rogercdavis.com. Good luck on your journey.

Glossary

Bull Market — a term used to describe market conditions in which stocks are moving higher.

Bear Market — a term used to describe market conditions in which stocks are moving lower.

Trend — the general direction of the market price of a stock or index. Trends can vary in length, and it's generally accepted that investing alongside the trend, and not against it, is a good way to enjoy profits and avoid big losers.

Secular — in this book the term is used to describe the long-term market structure. The market can be in a secular bull condition or a secular bear condition.

Cyclical — in this book this term is used to describe shorter-term trends that exist within the context of a longer-term trend. A cyclical bull market may exist inside a secular bear market.

Moving Average — a moving average is a mathematical expression of the relationship of a security's closing prices over some period of time. A ten-day moving average then is the average price of a security for the last ten days. If a security is trading above the moving average it can be said to be trending higher. The inverse would be said to be trending lower.

Price to Earnings Multiple (PE Multiple)— a mathematical expression of the relationship between a security's share price and its earnings. If a security has earnings per share of $1.00 and price of $20.00, the PE Multiple is 20. If the stock price drops to $15.00, the PE Multiple would be 15. This can be used as a valuation tool. If a stock has a high PE Multiple, some would say it's overvalued.

Exchange Traded Fund (ETF) — functions much like a mutual fund and is a way to gain exposure to a specific sector or other narrow area of the global market. Unlike a typical mutual fund, ETFs can be bought and sold intraday (funds can be traded only at the day's closing price).

Whipsaw — happens when a trading system gives a buy signal followed by a sell signal several times. It causes an investor to "buy high and sell low."

System — a set of trading rules that govern:
1. What securities to buy?
2. When to buy those securities?
3. How much of those securities to buy?
4. What to do with them as the future unfolds?

Disclosures

- Information presented is believed to be factual and up-to-date, but we do not guarantee its accuracy and it should not be regarded as a complete analysis of the subjects discussed. All expressions of opinion reflect the judgment of the authors on the date of publication and are subject to change.

- All information is based on sources deemed to be reliable, but no warranty or guarantee is made as to its accuracy or completeness. Financial calculations are based on various assumptions that may never come to pass. All examples are hypothetical and are for illustrative purposes only.

- No content should be construed as personalized investment advice nor should it be interpreted as an offer to buy or sell any securities mentioned. A professional advisor should be consulted before implementing any of the strategies presented.

- Past performance may not be indicative of future results. All investment strategies have the potential for profit or loss. Different types of investments involve varying degrees of risk, and there can be no assurance that any specific investment or strategy will either be suitable or profitable for an investor. In addition, there can be no assurances that an investor's portfolio will match or outperform any particular benchmark.

- The tax, legal, and estate planning information provided is general in nature. It should not be construed as legal or tax advice. Always consult an attorney or tax professional regarding your specific legal or tax situation.

- Asset allocation and diversification do not assure or guarantee better performance and cannot eliminate the risk of investment losses.

- Charts, graphs, and references to market returns, do not represent the performance achieved by any of the advisor's clients.